Innocent Victims

Poetic injustice in Shakespearean tragedy

By the same author
'LET WONDER SEEM FAMILIAR'
Endings in Shakespeare's romance vision

Innocent Victims
Poetic injustice
in Shakespearean tragedy

R.S. WHITE

THE ATHLONE PRESS, LONDON

This edition first published in 1986
by The Athlone Press Ltd
44 Bedford Row, London WC1R 4LY

Copyright 1982, 1986 R. S. White

Innocent Victims is a revised version of an edition privately printed in
1982

British Cataloguing in Publication Data
White, R. S.
Innocent victims : poetic injustice in Shakespearean
tragedy.——2nd ed.
1. Shakespeare, William——Characters
I. Title
822.33   PR2989

ISBN 0-485-11295-7

Library of Congress Cataloging in Publication Data
White, R. S., 1948–
Innocent Victims
Bibliography P   Includes index
1 Shakespeare, William, 1564–1616 – Tragedies
2 Shakespeare, William, 1564–1616 – Characters
I Title
PR2983.W46   1986   822.3'3   86–3538

ISBN 0-485-11295-7

Typesetting by Inforum Ltd, Portsmouth
Printed in Great Britain at the University Press, Cambridge

To the memory of
Dr Peter Laver
1947–83

Contents

Preface to second edition

I have taken the opportunity of making corrections to the first edition (published in 1982) and of adding some passages in each chapter in the light of the many helpful comments made by readers. In particular I should mention Professor Francis Berry, Dr Mark Corner, John Pellowe, Dr John Sloan, Dr David Norbrook and Jane Whiteley. My debts still remain to those acknowledged in the first edition, namely Dr Desmond Graham, Dr Linda Anderson, Peter Regan, Sally Woodhead, John Jowett, David Fishel and Ian Robson. I am also grateful to the editor of *Ariel* who permitted the republication in modified form of the essay on Ophelia. Many others helped by providing enthusiasm and support for my ideas, and without their encouragement I should not have contemplated this edition. Primary amongst these are the students in the English Department at the University of Newcastle upon Tyne, and my father, W.E. White.

I quote from Brecht by kind permission of John Willett, Michael Hamburger and Methuen London; from Dylan Thomas by permission of J.M. Dent Ltd; and from Walter de la Mare by permission of the Literary Trustees of his work and the Society of Authors as their representatives.

The first begetter of this edition was Dr Simon Silverman of the Humanities Press: his tragic death has robbed writers and the publishing world of a great deal of sympathetic energy. My thanks go to Brian Southam and The Athlone Press for kindly taking up the project.

February 1985   R.S. White

Innocent Victims
Poetic injustice in Shakespearean tragedy

One mode in which the dramatic exhibition of passion excites our sympathy without raising our disgust is, that in proportion as it sharpens the edge of calamity and disappointment, it strengthens the desire of good. It enhances our consciousness of the blessing, by making us sensible of the magnitude of the loss.

HAZLITT

The great secret of morals is love; or a going out of our own nature, and an identification of ourselves with the beautiful which exists in thought, action, or person, not our own. A man, to be greatly good, must imagine intensely and comprehensively; he must put himself in the place of another and of many others; the pains and pleasures of his species must become his own. The great instrument of moral good is the imagination; and poetry administers to the effect by acting upon the cause. Poetry strengthens the faculty which is the organ of the moral nature of man, in the same manner as exercise strengthens a limb.

SHELLEY

Blessed are the meek: for they shall inherit the earth.
Blessed are the peacemakers: for they shall be called the children of God.
Blessed are they which are persecuted for righteousness' sake: for theirs is the kingdom of heaven.
The Sermon on the Mount

The profoundest of all sensualities
is the sense of truth
and the next deeper sensual experience
is the sense of justice.

D.H. LAWRENCE

. . . justice, justice, justice, justice.
ISABELLA, Measure for Measure

I Fore Thoughts

Writers of tragedy often seem to be very profligate with human lives. Taking upon themselves the role of a god they create personages with recognizably human traits in whom we are encouraged to invest our understanding and sympathy, only to dispose of them later by killing them off, sometimes with not a little violence. In doing so, they would claim not merely to be flirting with our affections, nor imitating 'life' directly (for life, unfortunately, does not respect rules of predictability). In fact, they claim to be teaching us some moral lesson by showing us fictional examples. The theory runs that we are shown causal links between the way a person lives and how he or she is treated by the author at the end of the work, in such a way that each gets due deserts. Oscar Wilde's Miss Prism with an admirable succinctness sums up the theory at its simplest: 'The good ended happily, and the bad unhappily. That is what fiction means.'[1] If she were to give a name to her theory, she would call it poetic justice. To add just a little more complexity, we say that as a rule in literature the good prosper, the bad are punished, and (to cover the case of the sympathetic hero) the tragic protagonist, betrayed by some subtle moral flaw, is both punished and celebrated in a death which brings release from painful mental suffering. The rule works quite well in explaining the endings of comedies and tragedies alike. Lovers are united in marriage, villains are punished, and even the death of a tragic hero, which gives his life a rounded completeness, can lead us to reflect upon his particular kind of flawed greatness and to ponder upon how we can avoid such a fate. Nothing could be more instructive in its relentlessly retributory nature.

The trouble starts when we begin to ask a few questions based on our knowledge that outside literature moral problems can be open to profoundly differing judgments. Death may be inevitable, but does anybody *deserve* to die? To what extent can external, social and political forces be said to modify an impression that a person has 'invited' his or her own death, by indiscretion or personal weakness?

Is it not possible to 'learn' something about good and evil if we witness a murder, and if so then is it not the wickedness of the murderer rather than the victim's 'fatal flaw' that we notice primarily? Such a mode of questioning could be parried by the literary theorist by saying that it may be appropriate in our day-to-day lives but not when we are examining the more structured and rigorous, 'hypothetical' world of fiction and drama. But this surely leads straight into a trap. If we cannot raise questions about literature which are deeply troubling and relevant in life, then in what sense can the dramatist or theorist say that we are being taught? Any lesson we might draw from such a hermetically sealed and artificially controlled context is hardly worth the learning. Luckily, there is a way out of the trap, but the path leads in a lengthy direction away from any simple recognition of poetic justice in literature, and closer to a disturbing realization that poetic *injustice* may be just as instructive in drama as in life.

In Shakespeare's tragedies, generally acknowledged to be among the greatest examples of the genre, we find the rules of poetic justice operating in a superficial manner but also decisively broken. As well as the villains and the flawed tragic heroes, he gives us people who are patiently virtuous and even lovable, killed for no real fault. Only the sophist would claim that they are solely responsible for the sufferings they undergo, and the logic used would be the callous absurdity of those who argue that every rape victim has invited assault. In Shakespeare's case we may redefine the question. Is it not possible that such an assured dramatist, by including amongst his personages in each tragedy a clearly defined 'victim' is basically inviting us to contemplate the existence and nature of injustice itself, in order to stir in us a feeling of moral outrage that such events can be tolerated in any society? If so, then his wisdom and quiet moral instructiveness may reveal itself as even more subtle and broad than we had previously realized.

The argument of this book is that Shakespeare's 'victims' have not received justice even from the critics, since every book on Shakespearean tragedy that we can think of focuses upon the suffering of the tragic hero, barely noticing that other people suffer as well. Of course, the plays themselves partially encourage such an approach, for we must accept that *Macbeth* is primarily about Macbeth, *Othello* about Othello and so on, if only because these characters talk about themselves a lot. It is also true, however, that in the fluctuating experience through time of watching or reading a tragedy, there are moments of acute concentration upon others, when people whom we had 'thought too little on' suddenly arrest our attention, leaving us with powerful feelings that give us a different perspective on the play. It seems worth exploring what is happening at these moments, even at the risk of temporarily forgetting what one critic has ironically called the 'exclusive men's club'[2] of the tragic heroes who have, after all, been well served by commentators. It is partly our own preconception that 'tragedy' is the prerogative of the great man who undergoes suffering within, which leads us to neglect other characters who, although given less space and fewer words, suffer no less. Perhaps the neglect is silently justified also by the way such characters are treated by their own dramatic societies which cannot spare much time for lamenting the victims and which often have a vested interest in actually covering up certain specific social injustices. Although I do not pretend that the subject is more than a small corner of a very large field, I think it can be shown that Shakespeare was constantly and uniquely concerned with the fate of the innocent victim from his earliest experiments in tragedy, and that his attentiveness, if anything, increased. In plays which are amongst his last use of the tragic mode, he represents in the fates of Desdemona and Cordelia situations which invite feelings of unqualified outrage and deep examination of prevailing concepts of social or poetic justice, as well as the moral positives embodied in these characters. In these plays, the victim stands in equal dramatic significance with the hero, and deserves our full concentration.

We may respond in many ways to the sight of Shakespeare's suffering victims, but two primary feelings may be presumed. First, the thoughtful mind may be drawn to comprehend, with rejective anger, the brutality and malevolence in societies which create the conditions for injustice. Secondly, we notice in the attitudes to life expressed by each of the victims a quality of great beauty, a desire for harmony, justice and truthfulness in human dealings. Between these two feelings there lies a clear connection. Like all martyrs, they die that we may live more morally, since we see imaginatively not only the injustice but also its alternative. If the plays can awaken our moral imaginations to indignation and also to increased awareness of the beauty of an ethic based on emotional cooperation, then the fictional deaths of the victims are not futile but instructive and ennobling. Paradoxes lie in the fact that the strength of our outrage is a measure of how the play itself has initiated us into a moral education, for we come to recognize that although (or because) virtue has been defeated and physically destroyed, it survives even more strongly as an unquenchable spiritual principle. As Shelley has said, the great works of art, including Shakespeare's plays, 'have celebrated the dominion of love, planting as it were trophies in the human mind of that sublimest victory over sensuality and force.'[3] The characters may die unjustly, but what they represent lives on in the mind. Much the same could, of course, be said of the tragic heroes in these plays, but since we are not made so acutely aware of the injustice in their deaths, the quality they represent is rather more ambiguous. They may exhibit courage and endurance, but not pure innocence. Whereas our participation in the sufferings of the hero may show us more about the dark potential in ourselves and others for inflicting suffering, the deaths of the victims may help us to contemplate and train our own more altruistic impulses. This book then, is partly about the outrage stirred in us when we feelingly watch the perpetration of an injustice, and partly about the perception of potential peace, harmony and justice which is displayed in our shared recognition of injustice itself.

Before Shakespeare, we hardly have any problems concerning the gratuitously sacrificed victim, for although such characters exist in the works of Marlowe and Kyd,[4] they are spared little sympathy or attention by the writers, who unremittingly concentrate upon the tragic hero. It is Shakespearean tragedy which introduces and relentlessly re-introduces the person who manifestly does not deserve to die, investing the moment with a clear presentation of suffering. When we recall *Hamlet* and *Othello*, at least a part of our minds will remember the pity we felt on seeing Ophelia's distraction and on hearing Desdemona sing the willow song. In every tragedy by Shakespeare, alongside the tragic protagonist who is proclaimed by himself and others as a suffering centre, stands, sometimes silently, the figure of pathos who is a lamb of goodness: Lavinia, Ophelia, Desdemona, Cordelia, the children. There is enough in the plays to prove that Shakespeare is drawing our attention to these figures, inviting us to use our feelings as touchstones of truth. At the same time, there is also enough evidence to show that other characters in the plays are not paying attention, a fact which may confuse our interpretation.

Inevitably, a book which consistently adopts the point of view of the victim will be limited as a total approach to the great tragedies. There seems some point, however, in pursuing this particular bias, since the almost universal posture of orthodoxy amongst critics of the plays is based upon a prevailing, although usually unstated, admiration for the 'great man', which perhaps deserves to be questioned from time to time. Harriett Hawkins shares my view:

> At some point in the future, it may, and I devoutly hope it will, seem a waste of time to argue the case for characters who are so obviously the innocent victims of cruel injustice as Webster's Duchess and Chaucer's Griselda. Yet here and now, at least, it seems legitimate to do so in order to raise some critical questions about authority in general, and to show how academic efforts to moralize, condone, or rationalize even the most conspicuous forms of poetic injustice have resulted in a critical failure to do justice to works which cannot but elicit outraged protests against some specific forms of social and political injustice.[5]

It is revealing to glance at some of the forms in which academic rationalization have been expressed, for the critic himself may not even be aware that it is happening. In order that we may turn the more quickly to the subject itself, however, I have relegated to an Appendix an account of various attitudes adopted by other critics. In the meantime, we shall look more broadly at the place of victims in plays which superficially invite us to devote all our attention to a great man, the heroic protagonist. Then, in a set of essays which examine each in the context of the particular play, we turn to the particular characters. A pattern emerges in Shakespeare's developing modes of presentation of victim figures, from fairly straightforward cases towards more complex. Lavinia, Lucrece, and many of the innocent children who die in the tragedies, are shown as emblems of the suffering victim, presented in such a way that their fates allow us to recognize and analyse more acutely the deficiencies in the world of male and political dominance that is presented in each work. Ophelia is seen as an innocent and unformed person who is baffled and destroyed by the coercive powers of subterfuge, lying and indecision that mark Claudius's court, and which are equally troublesome to

Hamlet. The case of Desdemona is more complex still, for she shares an equal dramatic position with Othello and Iago, and cannot simply be dismissed as a minor or peripheral character. She is caught between two opposing concepts of 'justice', the one social and the other religious, and murdered needlessly for she is innocent throughout. The beauty of the ethic which she herself lives by, however, gives her the pyrrhic victory of the martyr, planting in our minds the trophies of love and goodness which Shelley emphasized. In the case of Cordelia, we can say that the question of her death is as much the source of tragedy in the play as Lear's, and her poetic destiny, largely a silent one, is to expose for us, more forcefully than anywhere else, the malign concentration in her society upon the tyranny of wordy people and of authority in general, a force which prevents the honest exercise of goodness and sympathetic feeling.

To avoid possible confusion, I should at the outset emphasize that this book will concern itself with *innocent* victims, and not address itself to the wider argument that even the guilty may be victims. It cannot be denied that Shakespeare has an unnerving way of taking us into the mind of even a villain and allowing us to comprehend that social victimization may have been a contributory factor in building up a personality. We remember the anti-semitism which hardens Shylock towards Christians, the ridicule of his deformed body which makes Richard III in his turn callous of others and hungry for power, we realize that Iago has a specific grudge against Cassio and Othello after being passed over for promotion, and we may interpret Lady Macbeth's ruthlessness in steeling her husband's purpose as a response to her personal ineffectuality in a masculine world. Most memorably, in *King Lear*, we are led to understand the vendetta against family and state held by Edmund as a result of ostracism introduced by his own father in harping on his son's illegitimacy:

> Thou, Nature, art my goddess; to thy law
> My services are bound. Wherefore should I
> Stand in the plague of custom, and permit
> The curiosity of nations to deprive me,
> For that I am some twelve or fourteen moonshines
> Lag of a brother? Why bastard? Wherefore base?
> When my dimensions are as well compact,
> My mind as generous, and my shape as true,

As honest madam's issue? Why brand they us
With base? with baseness? bastardy? base, base?
    (I.ii.1–10)[6]

Delivered to the audience in the intimacy of a soliloquy, such a vehement and eloquent statement must force us to find an understandable, if perverse 'legitimacy' in the disruptive actions of such a character later in the play. Even tragic heroes such as Othello and Lear may well be seen as 'more sinn'd against than sinning', and indeed, many critics bend over backwards to interpret the tragic hero's actions, however destructive, as a consequence of some kind of victimization. I do not wish to deny for a moment the validity of such an approach but merely to point out that beyond the 'guilty victims' there are also innocent ones, and to insist that the presence of the latter in each play is just as morally significant to our understanding. The extra, unfortunate point that should be made is that where the guilty victims have attracted the attentions of an unending number of sympathetic commentators, the innocent have always been consigned to the margins of critical scrutiny.

II Innocent Victims

In time of war, to take an extreme example, we sometimes use the word 'tragedy' to describe two different kinds of fate, which we should properly distinguish. There is the tragedy of the soldier on the front line, who chooses, or is chosen, to face the threat of death actively and directly. He may go in blindness, or reluctance, or idealism, or patriotism or even as an escape from a mundane and routine existence, but having entered the situation at least he knows the enemy, and knows the odds against him. To die as a hero for a cause, and even to die disillusioned with that cause, makes him into one kind of tragic protagonist, facing directly enormous but accepted odds, liberated from the daily habits of the life he has left. On the other hand, there is the tragedy of the civilian casualty. The women, children, pacifists and old men, those who happen to lie in the way of a bomb or an army, are no less tragic figures but of a different kind. They may be ones who have deliberately chosen not to take part in the soldier's debate with death, and yet they are deprived of the choice *not* to die as a consequence of war. Their deaths upon a lowly stalk represent not just grotesque bad luck; they are an inevitable consequence of the wilful decisions of others who claim to hold in their possession the welfare of ordinary citizens. The fate of the civilian casualties provokes no eulogy for courage and high-mindedness, but outrage at the cruel assumption adopted by others of power over life and death. They have their requiems, elegies of innocence and youth, but when the poets turn from the heroism of the front line to this group, they wear their rue with a difference, a note of shock mingled with the pity:

> I know not whether
> Adam or Eve, the adorned holy bullock
> Or the white ewe lamb
> Or the chosen virgin
> Laid in her snow
> On the altar of London,
> Was the first to die

In the cinder of the little skull.

Dylan Thomas, 'Ceremony After a Fire Raid'

Anguish at the waste of living things is common to both concepts of tragedy, but whereas the first celebrates individualistic courage, a measure of freedom to choose a situation which clearly involves the possibility of violent death, and confrontation with dangers outside the common run, the second represents a violation of the values of love, kinship, social decencies and domestic peace which are threatened by the existence of war itself. There may be no 'justice' in the death by war of either soldier or civilian, but at least there is some small degree of fairness, predictability, or 'poetic justice' for the former, and none for the latter. Those who live by the sword may die by the sword, but those who do not, should not.

The analogy is not anachronistic in a discussion of Shakespeare's tragedies, for he presents us with a similar distinction between concepts of tragedy. On the front line stand Lear, Hamlet, Othello, Macbeth; all statesmen, leaders, politicians and men involved with extreme conflict. They choose, or are chosen, to stand on our behalf as individuals against forces that are not so much social as metaphysical, martial and national. They implicitly acknowledge that the odds are death, simply by accepting their position in the state. On the other hand, Cordelia, Ophelia, Desdemona, Lady Macduff and the children, stand apart from this towering struggle, and seek to keep their worlds on a steady keel of quiet love, compassion and familial tenderness. Danger for them arises when they resist, or get in the way of, the front-line fighters. Just for a few minutes in each tragedy, Shakespeare turns our gaze towards the innocents, forcing us to notice, to feel shock and deep sense of injustice; but then the action resumes its course on the level of 'the fierce dispute 'twixt damnation and impassioned clay'[1]. The soldiers have chosen the priorities in these plays, and since they have the power, they cannot afford to let us linger too long over unfortunate accidents. In their own tragic intensity they draw attention to public struggles. But if we should demand the right to linger, and to give full force to such moments, we find ourselves in possession of an insight into the nature of a moral world presented in each play which threatens to upset the balance, forcing us to question many assumptions about the nature of suffering.

There is a servant who intervenes to prevent the blinding of
Gloucester, in *King Lear*, and his death is barely noticed by other
characters, in their red-toothed gloating upon cruelty:

Cornwall: See't thou shalt never. Fellows, hold the chair.
    Upon these eyes of thine I'll set my foot.
Gloucester: He that will think to live till he be old,
    Give me some help! – O cruel! Oh you gods!
Regan: One side will mock another; th'other too.
Cornwall: If you see vengeance –
1 Servant: Hold your hand, my lord.
    I have serv'd you ever since I was a child;
    But better service have I never done you,
    Than now to bid you hold.
Regan: How now, you dog!
1 Servant: If you did wear a beard upon your chin
    I'd shake it on this quarrel. What do you mean?
Cornwall: My villain!   [*They draw and fight.*
1 Servant: Nay, then come on, and take the chance of anger.
                                    [*Cornwall is wounded.*
Regan: Give me thy sword. A peasant stand up thus!
                [*She takes a sword and stabs him from behind.*
1 Servant: O, I am slain! My lord, you have one eye left
    To see some mischief on him. O!   [*Dies.*
Cornwall: Lest it see more, prevent it. Out vile jelly!
    Where is thy lustre now?
Gloucester: All dark and comfortless!
    (III.vii.66–84)

Painful as it is to contemplate this scene, the dramatist has given it to
us, and he invites us to adopt some attitude towards it. The one thing
we surely should not do is ignore it, or nod safely that 'life is like
that', pointing out comfortingly that the Servant in his righteous
anger has accepted the risk of being killed. Nor, I think, would any
sensitive person choose so to dismiss it. The incident provides us
with a supreme example where it is our own moral imaginations,
and nothing explicit in the play, which determine our immediate
response.

    The characters themselves, however, blatantly ignore it, to the
extent of saying loudly that their intention is to blind spectators to

the facts in front of them. Regan is not only blinding Gloucester, but herself and the others present, and she would seek in this gesture to blind us in the audience. Despite our best feelings, there may even be a sense in which she succeeds in this last aim, for the abrupt death of the Servant, and his sheer courage, are apt to be lost to the memory in the sick horror of the whole scene. The play goes on, and we are not allowed to dwell upon a moment which is largely irrelevant to the plot. As our moral judgments awaken after the first numbness, they harden into a condemnation of the blinding of Gloucester, but also bring a form of amnesia concerning our momentary concern for the Servant. It is only by deliberately *remembering* his impulsive outrage, anger and courage, that we can keep in our minds a firm sense of moral values which will allow us to recognize the constant and total deficiencies in the world of the play which allow such episodes to occur. The servant's gesture is a moral touchstone, allowing us to interpret and recoil from the blinding, but his action itself is almost forgotten. A messenger, faithful to his kind, reminds us, when reporting the death of Cornwall:

> A Servant that he bred, thrill'd with remorse,
> Oppos'd against the act, bending his sword
> To his great master; who, thereat enrag'd,
> Flew on him, and amongst them fell'd him dead;
> But not without that harmful stroke which since
> Hath pluck'd him after.
> (IV.ii.73–7)

But even the morally regenerated Albany virtually ignores the Servant's plight, finding a moral that hinges upon poetic justice, rather than the sense of injustice. He sees Cornwall's death as the gods' revenge for the blinding of Gloucester. If, however, we choose to notice and remember the Servant himself, we can sustain a perception which the event has awakened in us: that there is something terribly wrong and outrageous about a world in which such characters as Cornwall, Edmund, Goneril and Regan are allowed any authority whatsoever, and further, that authority itself, even in the figure of a master or the King, is intrinsically inferior, morally speaking, to conscientious and fully felt honesty of action. The perception leads directly on to a consideration of the more prominent victim, Cordelia. A warning that we must also take from the scene is that it is all too easy to forget our own perceptions, especially when the characters in the play itself not only neglect humane feelings, but try physically to blind others to them. In order that the 'teaching' function of the work of literature should operate, we must be prepared to question the wilful rationalizations and cover-up jobs perpetrated by the characters in authority, and hold on to these moving but fleeting moments when a deeply moral feeling is touched. In such cases we must trust our feelings, rather than the bulk of words in the play.

Another celebrated incident of brief but shocking victimization, taken as a test-case by Harriett Hawkins in the book already mentioned, is the death of Cinna the Poet in *Julius Caesar*. His is a slightly different case from the Servant's since he is not asserting any moral principle. His misfortune is to bear the name of a conspirator at a time when forces of mob destruction are on the streets:

> *3 Plebeian*: Your name, sir, truly.
> *Cinna*: Truly, my name is Cinna.
> *1 Plebeian*: Tear him to pieces; he's a conspirator!
> *Cinna*: I am Cinna the poet, I am Cinna the poet.
> *4 Plebeian*: Tear him for his bad verses, tear him for his bad verses!
> *Cinna*: I am not Cinna the conspirator.
> *4 Plebeian*: It is no matter, his name's Cinna; . . .
>   (III.iii.26–32)

In speaking of this episode, Hawkins, with characteristic incisiveness, says that, although it adds nothing to the main plot of the play, yet 'it contributes very significantly to the meaning and relevance of that tragedy':

> Within the larger context of Shakespeare's tragedy of state, Cinna can stand for all victims of mob violence, for all helpless victims of external forces over which they have no control, which they do not understand, and to which they have contributed nothing.[2]

Cinna differs from the Servant in *Lear* in ways which can hint at the variety of those people in Shakespeare's 'victim' class. The forces which destroy him are not those in properly instituted authority, but those which assert mass violence. The similar fates of the two, however can show us that the arbitrary tyranny of a master can be just as meaninglessly violent as that of a mob intoxicated with its own physical power. Indeed, in the context of *Julius Caesar* itself, the tacit message is obvious enough, that political action can be equally brutal and reprehensible, whether it comes from a high-minded idealist such as Brutus, a shrewd manipulator such as Antony, or a mindless mob. It is Brutus himself who has unleashed the dogs of mass violence, however principled his action may have been, and it is Antony who has stirred the mob to violence, as a huntsman goads his dogs. The death of Cinna shows us briefly but tellingly, in a way that no amount of didactic commentary could achieve, that political action taken on behalf of an ideal, a cause, a name (whether 'Caesar' or 'Brutus') will of its own nature be chaotic, destroy personality, privacy and ordinary life and create untold numbers of victims who happen to be in the way. We might detect in Shakespeare's artistic decision to make Cinna a poet by profession, a rueful comment that the poet, perhaps ineffectually, stands against such assertions of power, and thereby risks either the wrath of whoever is in power at a particular time, or else the distortion, misunderstanding, and under-valuing of his own perceptions.

If the victims are exploited by their societies, they are also, to a greater or lesser extent, exploited by the dramatist for particular functions. We are often encouraged to invest much positive feeling in some characters, so that the shock of seeing them swept aside by circumstances will be all the greater. It is a curious paradox that the more we know and love such a character, the more we are tempted to be impatient with his or her acceptance of victim status. We want them to assert themselves against the sea of circumstances, and reassure us of the possibility of individual freedom. We want to repeat to Desdemona and Ophelia Brecht's heartfelt advice:

And I always thought: the very simplest words
Must be enough. When I say what things are like
Everyone's heart must be torn to shreds.
That you'll go down if you don't stand up for yourself
Surely you see that.[3]

If we follow the line of reasoning, then, however well-intentioned, we draw closer to the critics who seek to *blame* such characters for their passivity, or even rationalize their deaths to assert personal responsibility, rather than understanding their attitudes to life. Desdemona, they say, is a liar and she disobeys her father. Cordelia is stubborn and perverse, Ophelia is rather stupid. It is necessary to resist such reasoning if the full dramatic function of the characters is to operate upon us. We must be cautious of trusting the voices of social propriety and expedience in these matters, for they will draw us into two fallacies. First, by judging the victims according to the standards of 'the world', and according to political expediency, we are falling into the trap of believing those in the plays who would seek to cover up, condone, and justify, every form of injustice. We are no better than Iago. Secondly, it should be recognized that the virtuous characters are not congenitally victims but they are congenitally and uncompromisingly *good*. They are incapacitated from acting in any other way by the inner demands of their characters. We shall see this point illustrated time and again, from the examples of Lucrece to Desdemona. They could act in no other way. When considering the case of the Servant in *Lear* for instance, we cannot simultaneously applaud him for his pure and decisively moral action, an expression of our own better feelings, and also regret his rashness, suggesting that impetuous folly made him responsible for his own death. Such a conclusion is falling in with the devil's party.

Of course, we can raise similar questions about the major tragic figures. We can debate about whether Lear, Macbeth, Othello and Hamlet are victims of circumstances, or whether they make responsible choices about their own destinies. The crucial difference lies in the fact that these characters have more than a measure of worldly power and authority which they all employ on occasions, for better or worse, in choosing destiny for themselves and the state. They are answerable not only to themselves but to those around them. The victims have no situational power, and they cannot fairly be judged as if, by their own decisions, they could have changed the course of events. Those who knowingly accept power over others are accepting a bargain. They must expect to be judged against far more stringent standards of personal responsibility than others. All Shakespeare's historical Kings, and especially the Henrys, IV, V, and VI, confront the dilemmas which beset the man of institutional power. There is a considerable amount of moral and political weight behind the Elizabethan axiom that if a ruler abdicates, or commits a sin, then the whole nation suffers. Although we could well see Shakespeare's tragedies as peopled entirely by victims (even Edmund was a bastard, and Iago had legitimate grudges), yet they all stand somewhere on a spectrum that reaches from the absolute powerlessness of Cinna the Poet towards the absolute power of a Claudius. The characters who are the subject of this book all stand upon the pole of powerlessness, and their status as victims is precisely what matters when we examine their histories. Whilst the fates of the major figures might show us there is something defective about their own characters and their use of power, the fates of the victims show us consistently that there is something very wrong in the world they live in, no matter how strenuously other characters try to ignore the defects or rationalize them. If we can learn to take the lessons shown to us about the cruelties and injustices of society, then although we cannot without insult say that the characters did not die in vain, we can say that the dramatist's exploitation of such characters is justifiable.

If the moments of poetic injustice operate in roughly the way which has been discussed, then one implication is that they force us marginally to devalue or at least detach ourselves to some extent from the sufferings of the central tragic protagonists, the 'front line fighters', whose deaths have a measure of poetic justice. This consequence is hardly surprising. If the bulk of the play's world neglects and ignores the victims which it creates, then by attending to the victim we must be sharply aware of deficiencies in those characters who most overtly claim authority over our attention. We need not dismiss the anguish of Lear, Hamlet, Macbeth and Othello as of no significance, for suffering is suffering, and should not be demeaned. But we can begin to re-assess the nature of their pain, and to place them in a different perspective. What can we say, then, by way of generalization about the nature of the suffering undergone by the main tragic heroes?

The classical answer, that the tragic hero is a man of greatness, a prince or warrior, who falls on low times, implies that those who are of a certain social or political status can claim an innate heroic grandeur which the rest of us do not share, and which we must admire from below. This, of course, will not serve in more egalitarian times, to explain the undeniable power of many tragedies. We must find some point of human sympathy with these figures, and a considerable measure of participation in their feelings. A more satisfactory answer may lie in the debatable, but eloquent assertion, 'He suffers most who suffers in the mind'. It is inner suffering, rather

than external persecution, that marks off the classical prototype for
the tragic hero from the more ordinary mortals around him, but it is
a form of suffering that invites identification from the spectators.
Oedipus Rex, for example, a play which is often taken to be a
paradigm for other tragedies, shows a man who, having sinned
inadvertently by killing his father and marrying his mother, is happy
in his ignorance. He suffers only when knowledge begins to dawn.
The rest of his tribe suffers more physically from famine and natural
disasters. These general pains are seen eventually as a direct outcome
of his own sins, which must be confronted before there can be
material prosperity for the state. Characterized by burning curiosity
about his own identity, Oedipus takes a compulsive, mental journey, brushing aside warnings that he would be happier if he chose to
remain in the dark:

> *Jocasta*: Fear? What has a man to do with fear?
>   Chance rules our lives, and the fate is all unknown.
>   Best live as best we may, from day to day,
>   Nor need this mother-marrying frighten you;
>   Many a man has dreamt as much. Such things
>   Must be forgotten, if life is to be endured.[4]

This is probably the most comforting answer if one is in a subjugated
and dependent situation, but it is to Oedipus's credit that he recognizes his responsibility towards the nation, and chooses to examine
his own spiritual condition. Acceptance of his inadvertently sinful
actions brings upon him the burden of guilt, and the suffering that
follows is both a punishment for him and also the source of his
nation's regeneration. Perhaps all people individually are sinners
during their lives, but for those who are placed by circumstances in a
position of power over others the personal faults or blindnesses of
the one are magnified to the degree of the number they control. They
are accountable in a way that others are not, and conversely, their
mental suffering 'should' no doubt increase, likewise when they are
forced to take responsibility for their own shortcomings. Oedipus
plucks out his eyes as a gesture towards obliterating the truth, but
this makes the suffering even more inward and painful. He returns to
the place of his birth, in order to die in shame and mental torture.
The whole action is presented in such a way that the spectator can
both identify with Oedipus's suffering, since we all to some extent

sympathize with anybody who is suffering, and also judge Oedipus, as commoners judge their king, subjects their ruler.

By accident or by emulation, English Renaissance tragedy duplicates this essential pattern, although inevitably it plays out variations. Doctor Faustus and Macbeth, for example, have knowledge and superior power respectively, and the 'heroes' must live through the suffering which such isolation, and full recognition of guilt, bring to them. King Lear, although he spends much of the play protesting with self-pity and impotent anger that he is a man more sinned against than sinning, suffers most by trying to avoid the guilty recognition that he has built his life upon false foundations, upon a word, authority. Demanding sycophancy from his nation and family, he has taken too little care of such conditions as poverty and silent love all his life, preferring instead to demand obedience by right of his station. When he humbly acknowledges his guilt, we can more sympathetically enter his state of suffering whilst still recognizing the retribution. Othello's true suffering comes not during his doubts about Desdemona's possible infidelity, which no reasonable person would possibly sympathize with, but when he comes to realize that he has stupidly and wrongly slaughtered an innocent person, and when, like Oedipus, he has the moral courage to paint his guilt in its darkest colours.

Another contemporary form of tragedy, revenge tragedy, illustrates the same kind of suffering in the central protagonist. Revenge tragedy (at its most unremitting in *Titus Andronicus*, and at its greatest in *Hamlet*), shows the suffering of one who accepts the moral quandary of fighting violence with violence, using assassination as a means of cleansing society of one sin, and thereby acquiring the guilt himself. In the state of Denmark, or any community where a wrong has not been righted, 'foul crimes' must infect the air like ghosts, until they are 'burnt and purg'd away' (*Hamlet* I.v.10–12), but since they cannot be purged by ghosts in purgatory the job must be done by living people, who thereby propagate the 'pollution'. Inevitably, in such a moral world, violence and wrongdoing can never end until, as in Yeats's *Purgatory*, the guilty fathers kill their sons in order to 'appease the memory of the living and the remorse of the dead'. The revenger's duty may seem to be active, but his suffering is as inward and spiritual as that of any other tragic hero. Again, we find in the presentation of the hero of a revenge tragedy, the characteristic doubleness which, I have suggested, marks a recurrent pattern of what we can call the tragedy of the great man. We can sympathize with the protagonist's dilemma and his inner suffering, but at the same time we see that his actions are chosen by himself. By identifying himself with a code of 'justice', in the name of revenge, he is aligning himself with a particular code of morality which may deny certain areas of feeling, and he risks an inner revenge taken by his conscience when he perceives that personal values have been neglected.

In Shakespearean tragedy, our attention is, then, most centrally engaged by the inner suffering of the person who has sinned, and whose actions implicate many other people in his society. The tragic protagonist becomes more isolated at each step of his lonely inner journey, cut off from social and emotional relationships, and eventually coming face to face with a solitary self:

> Who is it that can tell me who I am?
> (*King Lear*, I.iv.229)

> Alone I did it.
> (*Coriolanus*, v.vi.117)

> My way of life
> Is fall'n into the sear, the yellow leaf;
> And that which should accompany old age,
> As honour, love, obedience, troops of friends,
> I must not look to have; . . .
> (*Macbeth*, v.iii.22–6)

> O, I could tell you –
> But let it be.
> (*Hamlet*, v.ii.329–30)

Self-proclaimed villains are isolated from the outset, having chosen a lonely road, without ever having known the mutual support of love and friendship:

> I grow; I prosper.
> Now, gods, stand up for bastards.
> (*King Lear*, I.ii.21–2)

Then, since the heavens have shap'd my body so,
Let hell make crook'd my mind to answer it.
I have no brother, I am like no brother;
And this word 'love', which greybeards call divine,
Be resident in men like one another,
And not in me! I am myself alone.
    (*3 Henry VI*, v.vi.78–83)

At the margins of our attention, existing quietly and asking for no sympathy from their fellows, dwell the victims. Their lives represent a different ethical basis altogether. Whilst their more illustrious neighbours are taking the path from harmony to discovery of sin, guilt, suffering and foreseeable death, the potential victims exist in a more sociable framework. They yearn for relationship, social integration and community responsibility. The ethic depends upon words like 'brother', 'sister' and 'love'. They seek for an amplification of the self to include the feelings of others, and they do not look for control over their fellows. These are the people at the edge of the play, and yet at the centre of a personal tragedy standing for the principles and the basic optimism of comedy. Like the unfortunate, conscientiously objecting son of Tamburlaine, their pacifism and co-operation often cause their abrupt and untimely deaths.

These characters must hope that they are playing a part in a comedy. Like Kent, they have to believe that the miracles which misery sees may come to pass: 'Fortune, good night; smile once more; turn thy wheel' (*King Lear*, II.ii.160– and 168). Comedy, whose direction is away from individualism and isolation towards social harmony and identity within relationship, thrives on temporary injustice, disguise, mistaken identity and disorientating journeys, safe in the certainty that all will be retrieved in final recognition and integration in the haven of the happy ending. The victims in tragedy have no option but to hope that this will happen. The servant in *Lear* reminds his master of the terms of 'service', and he evokes all the values of brotherhood and justice which would, one could confidently expect, be eventually heeded in the sanity of a comic world. The poet in *Julius Caesar* desperately hopes that he is caught in a comic situation, where mistaken identity will be cleared up in waves of laughter. Such hopes, which may be momentarily shared by the audience, are proved to be ineffectual and irrelevant, since they are appeals to a code incompatible with the tragic pattern. When the active, violent and individualistic pattern of tragedy is established, it is inevitable that those who represent the values of mutuality, sympathy and relationship — the comic values — get in the way, they are destined for the status of innocent victims.

In recognizing that the 'victims' to some extent belong more to a comic, benevolent world than to the world of the tragic hero, we can make an important distinction between what I have called 'great man' tragedy on the one hand, and love-tragedy on the other. (At this stage I am taking *Othello* to lie in the former category, although this must obviously be qualified.) It is significant that both Romeo and Antony, during the course of their respective plays, are trying to turn their backs on the demands of worldly society and the state. Romeo rebels against family concerns, and Antony has shed much of his military and political power in Rome. There are, of course, legions of critics quick to agree with the values of the military world, condemning the change in Antony's priorities as a fatal weakness. The triple pillar of the world is transformed into a strumpet's fool: 'Off with his head!'[5] This is to ignore the complexity, and moral validity, of the choice such characters have made. In their commitment to love, to sensuality and relationship, Romeo and Juliet, Antony and Cleopatra, have knowingly chosen what they see as a superior, more generous ethic, and they have rejected the individualistic concerns of a world based upon conflict, politics, statecraft, competition and hatred. They have chosen comedy as their field. Unfortunately, they find themselves trapped by the worlds which they previously inhabited, societies acting according to vindictive and violent values. Pinned like butterflies, the lovers themselves become the prime victims. The warring families and hostility in the city are the forces that destroy the bodies of Romeo and Juliet (but not their love), whilst the militaristic and imperialistic priorities represented by Rome will not leave Antony and Cleopatra to rest in their choice, and will eventually destroy them (but again, not their love). Like the victims in other plays, these lovers have the misfortune to stand in the way of prevailing ideologies which determine what is 'important' in the eyes of society. It is significant that Shakespeare's immediate successors in the field of tragedy should make the point even more obvious, as if Shakespeare has cleared the way for a starker perception into such victimization of people who choose to base their lives upon love. Webster in *The Duchess of Malfi* gives us a shining and glorious example of a woman who chooses love before duty and social propriety. The insane violence of those around her, who eventually destroy her, is presented in the harshest light possible. Ford's Annabella in *'Tis Pity She's a Whore* holds the same position of untainted purity, even as she breaks the social taboo of incest. Although the role of her brother Giovanni is equivocal, the whole presentation is remorselessly calculated to provoke us into condemning not only the hatred and brutality of the society, but also the hypocrisy and moral crudeness of the clergy who claim to speak for morality. It is perhaps in the nature of love-tragedy (as in another great example, *Tess of the d'Urbervilles*), that a lover who seeks for peace and harmony within a relationship is likely to become a victim of the forces of hatred and conflict in the surrounding society. This is certainly true of the plays which are among the first in this genre, *Romeo and Juliet* and *Antony and Cleopatra*.

I do not propose in this book to deal with these illustrious lovers, for they are themselves the leading tragic protagonists in their plays, as well as being victims. But we might pause to notice by the way, that even in these plays there are other, more unobtrusive victims, whose fate adds weight to our condemnation of the dominant societies. Both Mercutio and his kinsman, Paris, are good-hearted, loyal and loving, and these better feelings draw them into the destructive web of circumstances which destroy the lovers. It is a tragic irony that it is Romeo himself who kills Paris and directly contributes to the death of Mercutio by coming between his friend and Tybalt as they fight, thinking 'all for the best'. To this extent we are led to recognize that violence and conflict taint the consequences of the central love relationship, since it is enacted in a violent world. 'A plague a both your houses!'[6] is the most devastating and true condemnation made during the play. Similarly, Enobarbus is loyal and loving to his master, and he dies also partly as a result of tensions created by the love relationship. Without knowing it, Antony places his friend in a quandary between the old ethics of military success and expedience, and Enobarbus's own inbuilt feelings of devoted loyalty, analogous to Antony's newly acquired love. Enobarbus eventually commits suicide in remorse for betraying the latter principle. Again, however, we cannot condemn Antony, since he too has thought 'all for the best', and the real point to notice is that Enobarbus's predicament is precisely the one imposed upon Antony himself. Perhaps the lover becomes marginally tainted by the sins of the world in which he is forced to act, but the real enemy to Antony, Cleopatra and Enobarbus is the existence of the rival values of public, military morality. The fates of the unsung victims, Mercutio, Paris and Enobarbus parallel, and emphasize, the destinies of the central victims. In allowing us to see clearly the malevolence of a prevailing ethic which will not allow peace and love to exist quietly, their situations perform the same dramatic and instructive functions as the innocent victims in other tragedies.

Before we turn to the plays, one potential criticism of the argument proposed in this book must be squarely faced. It is often regarded as an exercise in anachronism to read back into works of a previous age our own, modern values of morality. The evidence shows that Elizabethan life was full of public cruelty, with bearbaiting, Bedlam, hanging and quartering of felons, the stocks, and the display of executed pirates by the sides of the Thames. Surely, runs the argument, the times were too brutal to foster a dramatist with a humane social conscience capable of acknowledging the vulnerability of the suffering? Surely we are sentimentalizing Shakespeare by suggesting that death, mutilation and rape are more than sensational stage events to please the groundlings? Such a blatant statement of objection can be easily parried by pointing out that throughout history there have been some people able to see and analyse the injustices and hypocrisies of their own societies. In England there is the example of Sir Thomas More, whose *Utopia* anatomizes a host of inequalities which still remain with us, and there must have been enough sympathizers in Elizabeth's court to initiate radical poor laws which were the 'foundation of a system of care and relief'.[7] A dramatist's job is to give voices to opposing moral viewpoints, and Shakespeare above all has been celebrated for his capacity to do just this. In one play he can show us a king insisting on the authority of his position and the same man perceiving a very different reality:

> Poor naked wretches, wheresoe'er you are,
> That bide the pelting of this pitiless storm,
> How shall your houseless heads and unfed sides,

Your loop'd and window'd raggedness, defend you
From seasons such as these? O, I have ta'en
Too little care of this! Take physic, pomp;
Expose thyself to feel what wretches feel,
That thou mayst shake the superflux to them,
And show the heavens more just.
    (*King Lear*, iii.iv.28–36)

Words like 'just' and 'justice' ring loud throughout the tragedies, not in any isolated literary sense of what the rules of writing decree but in a more urgent, concerned context of what constitutes fair dealing in society. Whatever Shakespeare's attitudes may have been, the plays stand by themselves as containing dramatically powerful moments when our own desire for justice is brought into play.[8] Most characteristically, these moments occur when we are asked to witness and contemplate figures of suffering virtue. It would be patronizing and self-deluding to say that we in the twentieth century (with our record of two disastrous wars and preparations for another) are the first people morally fastidious enough to respond to such moments with a liberal and enlightened conscience. To give a moderate answer to the charge of anachronism, we might bear in mind the words of one recent critic, G.K. Hunter:

> There is a danger, of course, in imputing modern squeamishness to an Elizabethan play; but there is also the danger of suppressing Shakespeare's human responses lest they seem too humane.[9]

Hunter is speaking here of a play which is certainly not for the squeamish, *Titus Andronicus*, and it is to this that we now turn.

III Lavinia

We do not need to make any particularly unorthodox claims for the genesis or quality of *Titus Andronicus* to suggest that in this play we find for the first time the pattern of tragic priorities which will serve Shakespeare for the rest of his writing career. Without attempting to place any particular evaluation on the play as a whole, the various ingredients of Shakespearean tragedy, as they have been proposed, can be fairly formally stated.

The dramatic concentration, more or less throughout, is upon the mental suffering of Titus as a person of authority. He is the military hero, favourite of the people, awarded the chance to settle the succession of the emperor of the state, and generous and legalistic enough to bestow it upon Saturninus as the rightful inheritor. He then spends the rest of the play seeing his own family literally and metaphorically dismembered, partly, it should be added, by himself, since he kills one of his sons and also his daughter, Lavinia. The kind of suffering he undergoes is mental and emotional rather than physical, since the loss of his hand is initially interpreted as, if anything, a relief, and no pain is registered. Titus is the person given the most truly moving and arresting poetry, as he gives voice to his suffering, and he acts with 'honour' throughout. Most of his suffering, however, can be traced back to his own actions, when he authorizes the death of Tamora's son, thus stirring her to revenge, and when he kills his own son, Mutius. He describes the latter incident as a 'brawl' (i.i.353), but it could equally be seen as Titus's unconsidered response to a genuine resistance on the part of all his sons upon seeing their sister used cynically as a political commodity when Titus agrees to her betrothal to the new emperor. In short, if we weigh up the debits and credits in the moral deserts of Titus, we find them pretty evenly balanced, or even tilted towards the debit side. And yet since he claims for himself the most vocal and eloquent expression of suffering, we accept him as worthy of attention as the tragic protagonist. We anticipate his death, find it poetically just, and also fairly moving.

The most important element in the Shakespearean tragic pattern for the purposes of this book, is the existence of several innocent victims, most starkly exemplified in Lavinia. They are at best exploited by the plot, at worst redundant to it. Their basic function is not primarily narrative, but to awaken our moral sympathies and attune our point of view, if we are not cauterized totally by the general tone of brutality and moral indifference that characterizes a society which is little better than a 'wilderness of tigers' (III.i.54). The first victim is Alarbus, Tamora's first-born son, a hapless man whose only fault is to be 'the proudest prisoner of the Goths' (I.i.96) and who, according to Roman ritual after war, must be sacrificed. Bassianus is marginally less innocent, since he is ambitious and politically motivated, but Mutius, Titus's youngest son, is guilty only of trying to protect his sister's emotional affiliations. Quintus and Martius, the other younger sons, do nothing wrong, and they are murdered simply because they are related to Titus, who has initially invoked the vengeful wrath of Tamora, aided by her black-hearted paramour, Aaron. The bastard child of Aaron and Tamora, who is killed later, is also innocent. His colour betrays his paternity, which taints him in the eyes of others by association. In a particularly gruesome image, Aaron describes his virtually gratuitous execution of the Nurse who had brought his child to him:

> Weeke weeke!
> So cries a pig prepared to the spit.
> (IV.ii.146–7)

The thoroughly guilty ones are those who undertake murder for motives of revenge: Tamora, Aaron, Tamora's sons, Saturninus (who kills Titus after the murder of his wife), and even by a hair's breadth, Titus himself. The only way in which we can adjudicate amongst the moral deserts is to conclude that the play condemns the rough justice of revenge itself. A society which acts on such a principle is revealed as morally trapped in a spiral of destructiveness which will never end until the ethic itself is challenged and outlawed. Unfortunately, nothing at the end of the play reassures us that this will happen. The surviving ruler, Lucius, is just as brutal and vindictive as anybody:

> As for that ravenous tiger, Tamora,
> No funeral rite, nor man in mourning weed,

> No mournful bell shall ring her burial;
> But throw her forth to beasts and birds to prey.
> Her life was beastly and devoid of pity,
> And being dead, let birds on her take pity.
>   (v.iii.195–200)

This, after the woman herself at the beginning of the play had pleaded for her son's life with exactly the appeals to parental love and protectiveness which Titus consistently invokes:

> Gracious conqueror,
> Victorious Titus, rue the tears I shed,
> A mother's tears in passion for her son;
> And if thy sons were ever dear to thee,
> O, think my son to be as dear to me!
>   . . .
> Thrice-noble Titus, spare my first-born son.
>   (i.i.104–8 and 120)

Nothing was learned at the beginning, and nothing acknowledged at the end. No other Shakespearean tragedy ends on such a note of mutual hatred, for the others conclude with some kind of eulogy. The one piece of faint good fortune for the Roman society and for Lucius is that he is the last remaining member of the two ruling families. Without a radical re-examination of its fundamental assumptions about 'justice' (a word that rings repeatedly, and hollowly, through the play), no other conclusion seems adequate in such a relentlessly revenge-centred society.

If we were to assume that Shakespeare intends us to 'enjoy' the brutalities in this play, it would be possible for us to condemn him for condoning such slaughter of innocent people in the interests of a sensational plot. An army of critics do indeed make this accusation, not on moral grounds but on aesthetic, since they feel that such '*grand guignol*' does not make for interesting art.[1] However, seen as a totality the play does not allow such a simple response, for then the close and feeling attention given to Lavinia would be irrelevant. The only sensitive attitude from an outside onlooker to her plight is a sickened and decisive rejection of the whole society which allows such things to happen, and this is the response encouraged by the whole presentation of the action.

Shakespeare often attaches to his victim an image which tells us much about the character's relationship with the social and moral world of the play. In the case of Lavinia, there are two main images, the first classical and literary, the second more visual. The resemblances between her story and the Ovidian tale of Philomel, are almost too obvious to need statement, but with a repetitive thoroughness that marks Shakespeare's earlier work, he emphasizes and reiterates the parallel, lest it go unnoticed:

> Fair Philomel, why she but lost her tongue,
> And a tedious sampler shew'd her mind;
> But, lovely niece, that mean is cut from thee.
> A craftier Tereus, cousin, hast thou met.
> And he hath cut those pretty fingers off
> That could have better sew'd than Philomel.
>   (II.iv.38–43)

Titus: Lucius, what book is that she tosseth so?
Boy: Grandsire, 'tis Ovid's Metamorphoses;
       My mother gave it me.
Marcus: For love of her that's gone,
       Perhaps she cull'd it from among the rest.
Titus: Soft! So busily she turns the leaves! Help her.
       What would she find? Lavinia, shall I read?
       This is the tragic tale of Philomel
       And treats of Tereus' treason and his rape;
       And rape, I fear, was root of thy annoy.
           (IV.i.41–50)

The main effect of the literary reference on the characters in the play is to turn their feelings into directed anger, and when they discover the names of the felons, the Andronici swear a terrible oath, invoking another classical myth, that of Lucrece, to revenge the rape with 'blood' (IV.i.85–95). The audience must also be compelled by the sense of outrage, which is enough 'To stir a mutiny in the mildest thoughts, And arm the minds of infants' (IV.i.86–7). The other image draws attention more specifically to the victim-status of Lavinia herself, and creates pathos rather than anger. Before the rape and dismemberment, she is described on several occasions as a doe, pursued by hunters. There is in fact a literal hunt going on, and significantly, Titus himself is enjoying it:

> The hunt is up, the morn is bright and grey,
> The fields are fragrant, and the woods are green.
> Uncouple here, and let us make a bay,
> And wake the Emperor and his lovely bride,
> And rouse the Prince, and ring a hunter's peal,
> That all the court may echo with the noise.
>   (II.ii.1–6)

The occurrence of a hunt in this tragedy is interesting, because, as I have argued elsewhere,[2] there is a very large amount of evidence to suggest that Shakespeare and his contemporaries associated the metaphor with comedy, to demonstrate the ambiguity of the 'love-hunt'. In *Love's Labour's Lost*, *The Taming of the Shrew*, *As You Like It*, *A Midsummer Night's Dream* and *Venus and Adonis* we find specific hunts, while plays like *Twelfth Night*, *Much Ado About Nothing* and *The Merry Wives of Windsor* are laced with references to different kinds of hunting. On balance, in these comedies the element of pursuit in relationships is accepted as a relatively healthy and harmless part of wooing. In *Titus Andronicus*, however, the humanist attitude towards hunting as a brutal activity is the one primarily presented. The hunt in *Titus* is in itself fairly harmless, but even Titus comes to regret it, for it marks the disaster which befalls his daughter, and the frequency of occasions on which the two events are connected shows the artist's intention:

> What, hast not thou full often struck a doe,
> And borne her cleanly by the keeper's nose?
>   (II.i.93–4)
> My lords, a solemn hunting is in hand;
> . . .
> Single you thither then this dainty doe,
> And strike her home by force if not by words.
>   (II.i.112–18)

> *Titus*: And I have horse will follow where the game
>   Makes way, and run like swallows o'er the plain.
> *Demetrius*: Chiron, we hunt not, we, with horse nor hound,
>   But hope to pluck a dainty doe to ground.
>   (II.ii.23–26)

There are other references to the destructive events in the forest which link them with the hunt, particularly in likening Lavinia to the doe or deer which is hunted and maimed, but enough evidence has been given to show that the metaphor is fully considered and deliberate. It is most disturbing because it is we in the audience who notice. The characters in the literal hunt for animals are convinced that they are engaged in a healthy, celebratory and sociable activity. We are alert to the fact that beneath the respectable façade of the occasion, another more deadly hunt is being pursued. The effect is twofold. Our private perception into the pathos of Lavinia's situation is stirred by prior knowledge, and intensified by the happy ignorance of her father. Secondly, Titus's enthusiastic endorsement of the hunt itself rubs off dangerously on his general attitudes, for morally speaking he is just as much implicated in the predatory ethic of Rome as it is presented in this play as anybody else, and he is to become even more purposefully a hunter of men and women as time goes on. The fact that it is he who eventually kills Lavinia, admittedly not in anger but in grief, confirms the existence of his own pollution from the social disease. These are the perceptions created in us by the rape of Lavinia in the woods, and their general import is to distance us morally from all the other figures of authority in the play, and condemn their world and their norms of justice.

Lavinia herself is hardly given enough lines to establish a fully developed personality in our minds, and in this she somewhat anticipates Shakespeare's presentation of Ophelia. All her speeches before the rape show her to be docile to her father's wishes, but spirited in her loyalty to the new emperor, when she condemns Tamora's adultery. After the rape, she is a bleeding, silent witness to the general evil of Rome. It is an insult to her plight that she is often used by other characters to justify their own self-centred desires for revenge and, as in the case of her uncle Marcus and her father Titus, their wordy insight into the wordlessness of true grief:

Marcus: O brother, speak with possibility,
And do not break into these deep extremes.
Titus: Is not my sorrow deep, having no bottom?
Then be my passions bottomless with them.
Marcus: But yet let reason govern thy lament.
Titus: If there were reason for these miseries,
Then into limits could I bind my woes.

When heaven doth weep, doth not the earth o'erflow?
If the winds rage, doth not the sea wax mad,
Threat'ning the welkin with his big-swol'n face?
And wilt thou have a reason for this coil?
I am the sea; hark how her sighs do blow.
      (III.i.215–27)

It will be noted time and time again, that the plight of the victim in Shakespeare's tragedies has at least the value of stirring other characters to deep and active feeling, and in this sense the unfortunate characters do not suffer totally without effect. However, in this play the feelings lead to angry and vindictive action. One other capacity of Lavinia should not go unnoticed, for it points forward to Cordelia. Even when deprived of speech, she is capable of eloquent gestures of fellow-feeling and love, sometimes acknowledged and sometimes not, and to this extent she provides the only gestures in this bloody, dark play that could be described as beautiful:

Titus: O, here I lift this one hand up to heaven,
      And bow this feeble ruin to the earth;
      If any power pities wretched tears,
      To that I call! [*To Lavinia*] What, would'st thou kneel with me?
      Do, then, dear heart . . .
            (III.i.207–11)

Lucius: An, that this sight should make so deep a wound,
      And yet detested life not shrink thereat!
      That ever death should let life bear his name,
      Where life hath no more interest but to breathe!
                                    [*Lavinia kisses Titus.*
Marcus: Alas, poor heart, that kiss is comfortless
      As frozen water to a starved snake.
Titus: When will this fearful slumber have an end?
            (III.i.247–5)

The spectacle of Lavinia, raped, bleeding, her arms and tongue cut off, and her death at the hands of her father, pull against our full acceptance that the tragedy is Titus's alone. Hers is a different kind of tragedy, no less affecting and horrifying than her father's. Without Lavinia, we would not be able to see the play as more than expressing an enjoyment of cruelty. Her fate acts as a powerful moral check upon our endorsement of the integrity of the Roman society as it is presented, and it allows us to know what the play shows us: that a world based on a revenge ethic is intrinsically unjust. It is a strong and clear 'moral' that could be appended to this hardened play. Although there is nobody on hand to interpret for us the simultaneous ugliness and beauty in these moments — we have no Gertrude, Emilia or Kent — yet when played upon the stage there could be nothing if not intense pathos, which is capable of stirring in us a feeling that the violation is not only directed at the body of a woman, but at a whole ethic of goodness and love which is fleetingly evoked in these touching incidents, but otherwise excluded.

Despite the absence of a truly sympathetic voice raised on Lavinia's behalf, it is possible to find in the play a running discussion of rival conceptions of 'justice' which implicitly place her in the role of a casualty of public morality. From the opening, Titus is characterized as a man identified with an unquestioning allegiance to Roman 'honour', a programmed code which impels him on a course observing ancient social and legal customs based on values of primogeniture set above moral authority, stoicism set above compassion, and revenge set above mercy. It is difficult to 'blame' such a consistent and honourable functionary of state justice, for there are no alternative values available to Titus in his society. His own rebellion, when he radically questions the notions of justice which he has been practising, comes with devastating swiftness from a recognition of the violation of a more private, perhaps more absolute sense of justice. In Act III, Scene ii, he dines with the poor remains of his family, and he makes much of the pathetic helplessness of Lavinia. The young boy, Lucius, weeps to see the general suffering and the scene is loaded with sentiment. It is at this moment that his brother Marcus kills a fly with his knife, only to be reprimanded:

> *Titus*: Out on thee, murderer, thou kill'st my heart!
> Mine eyes are cloy'd with view of tyranny;
> A deed of death done on the innocent
> Becomes not Titus' brother.
> (III.ii.54–7)

On being reminded, however, that the fly is as black as the Moor whose lover authorized the dismemberment of his innocent daughter, Titus snaps:

> O, O, O!
> Then pardon me for reprehending thee,
> For thou hast done a charitable deed.
> Give me thy knife, I will insult on him,
> Flattering myself as if it were the Moor
> Come hither purposely to poison me.
> There's for thyself, and that's for Tamora.
> . . .

(III.ii.68–74)

From this point onwards, Titus acts in a way that shows his moral sensibility to be cauterized, and he sets in motion his own ghoulish course of revenge. His breakdown in this scene is precipitated by the realization that any law of natural justice based on revulsion at the killing of a fly is simply incompatible with the public code of justice in Rome which he has implicitly accepted in condoning the revenge on the Goths which has in turn led to the attack on his family. However kind and dutiful a man, Titus is unregenerate in that he has initiated a spiral of self-destruction, a chain of vendettas which will continue until all implicated parties have been wiped out. In the total structure of the narrative, then, Shakespeare is not endorsing revenge as an ethic in the way that Seneca had, but he is showing up the futility and destructiveness of revenge, pointing out that it is contrary to natural justice.[3] Titus is a kind of victim in the process since he could hardly have visualized the consequences of his early actions, but he chooses to play out the full scenario of revenge thereafter. The truly innocent character who suffers most is Lavinia. It is in his emphasizing of her helpless distress that Shakespeare most clearly signals that in this play he is much less indebted in his moral vision to Seneca than to Ovid with that poet's 'tenderness in the midst of horror'.[4] *Titus Andronicus* has always been regarded as a Senecan, revenge tragedy, and judged in the terms of that brutal genre, but by paying attention to Lavinia we discover that its moral basis is quite contrary to Seneca, a challenge to any concept of justice which is grounded upon adherence to public codes of honour, and an incitement towards contemplation of a more absolute, 'natural' form of justice. The appropriate comparison is with *Timon of Athens*, another fundamentalist attack on expectations of justice based on the state's security (in the case of Alcibiades) and on money.

We do not need to linger over *Titus Andronicus*, since there are more important things in store. In this play Shakespeare is not simply reproducing a typical Senecan tragedy of revenge, and he is certainly not encouraging his audience to accept the action in some spirit of sadistic excitement and *frisson*. The presence of Lavinia allows us strongly and rationally to reject the ethic of revenge that marks this society, for the sight of her silent suffering can only harden us towards the others. It also allows us to resist the tug of Titus himself upon our sympathies, for although we see him as a sufferer himself, mouthing his emotional pain in eloquent fashion, yet he is also placed within the prevailing norm of justice. In this play, by introducing the truly innocent victims, Shakespeare is creating a blueprint for each of his tragedies to come. When critics speak of a grain of bitterness in the vision of *Troilus and Cressida*, they need not see it as anything particularly new in Shakespeare. In all his tragedies, beginning with *Titus Andronicus*, he is inviting us to feel anger and disgust at dominant attitudes of a society (whether it be Rome, Venice, Denmark or ancient England), whilst at the same time allowing us to recognize the heroes as sympathetic but none the less implicated people. He forges such a comprehensive medium of tragedy by developing the moral function of the innocent victim, the first of whom is Lavinia.

IV Lucrece

Titus Andronicus and *The Rape of Lucrece*, written within a few years of each other, have many resemblances. In particular, they both have at the centre a woman who is raped. Both show starkly that Shakespeare's literary interest in the innocent victim began more or less when he began writing tragedy. Taken together, the works give us a thorough presentation of the victim's predicament, caught between the internal demands of a sensitive and fastidious conscience, and the conditions of a brutal and authoritarian society.

Whereas Lavinia exists in a dramatic work, in which speech is the most accessible communicative gesture, Lucrece is placed in a poetic narrative which gives us insight into her thoughts and feelings. Lavinia is silenced by having her tongue torn out, and Lucrece is metaphorically silenced, by feeling that her situation is too shameful to be spoken of. They are in the same situation, but we can inevitably know more of Lucrece's feelings than Lavinia's. *The Rape of Lucrece* provides us with two crucial insights into the personality and predicament of the innocent victim. First, there is an unbearable and overwhelming inner torment that cannot be publicly expressed, and which centres on the dark psychological state of shame. Secondly, by a tacit but powerful implication from the narrative, and from a crucial narratorial intrusion, we should recognize that the victim is created by her social circumstances and by the attitudes and actions of those around her, which lead her into the self-destructive feelings of shame. More generally, the reader's moral sympathies are crucially tested, and to some extent tricked, into believing that society is right, the victim is wrong, simply because there is more expedient rationality and vocal self-justification on the side of society; more silence, self-recrimination, and apparent irrationality on the side of the isolated and frightened individual. The woman's consciousness tells her that she is somehow in error, and she kills herself in shame. On the other hand, there is more than enough evidence to suggest that she has been forced into a false position, and that she has no cause to blame herself, for Tarquin, and more or less all the other self-proclaimed commentators in the poem, are working from self-justificatory and destructive premises which demand our rejection.

Lucrece is initially placed in the position of victim by an event, the rape perpetrated upon her body by Tarquin. At this level of narrative and overall moral reflection, the poem is clear and unambiguous. Tarquin acts with evil and compulsive intention, whilst Lucrece is completely innocent. He, protected from self-knowledge and from the world's condemnation of the 'pleats of majesty' (line 93) which attached to this position of authority, does the deed in lust. He forfeits any sense of personal virtue, 'And for himself himself he must forsake' (157). Heedless of the consequences, he assumes that 'misty night Covers the shame that follows sweet delight' (356–7), and even afterwards the sense of shame which breaks over him like an ocean wave owes more to his fear of losing his honour and reputation than a true sense of guilt. When he ruminates 'Shameful it is — ay, if the fact be known' (239), the afterthought gives away his real preoccupation. There is some degree of self-awareness in the knowledge that 'his soul's fair temple is defaced' (719) as he slinks away into the darkness, but the poet, by switching attention away from Tarquin to Lucrece, allows us no sympathy for the evil-doer who has violated the body and soul of a human being. It is a curious and, I think, telling fact that the commentators on the poem seem to lose interest at this point. Obsessed as they are with the psychological state of the 'great man', they are excited to find similarities between Tarquin, Macbeth and Othello, but find little of interest in the remaining 1100 lines of the poem, dismissing it as turgid rhetoric.[1] It must be obvious that such an approach pulls against the whole design of the poem.

The real point of the narrative is to explore the psychological state of the victim after the event. It is not wholly relevant to the execution of the poem itself to brood upon the classical paradox associated with Lucrece's feelings '*Si adulterata, cur laudata? Si pudica, cur occisa?*'[2] No doubt Lucrece's contemplation of her situation and feelings is riddled with logical errors and false premises, but the poem is not pretending to present a consistent philosophical position. Instead, it demonstrates a complex, confused, and real emotional state — the strange and deep sense of shame acquired by the victim herself after the evil actions of another. The narrator's point of view weaves in and out of the tortured consciousness of Lucrece, in a way that makes the poem more like a phantasmagorical nightmare than a story.

Before we examine Lucrece's emotional state, it is necessary to repeat that at the most obvious level of the poem the moral bearings are firm and consistent. We cannot see the woman as anything but a victim, even before the rape when 'Like to a new-kill'd bird she trembling lies' (457). She is constantly presented as a person of 'virtue' and, indeed, 'a virtuous monument' embodying the beauty of inviolate nature:

> Her eyes, like marigolds, had sheath'd their light,
> And canopied in darkness sweetly lay,
> Till they might open to adorn the day.
>   (397–9)

After the rape, her victim-status is emphasized by the repeated analogy to the myth of Philomel, as in *Titus Andronicus*. She sings,

> 'Come Philomel, that sing'st of ravishment,
> Make thy sad grove in my dishevell'd hair.'
>   (1128–9)
> 'And for, poor bird, thou sing'st not in the day,
> As shaming any eye should thee behold.'
>   (1142–3)

The nightingale, the metamorphosed Philomel, sings tongueless in the solitude of darkness, bewailing a shame so private that it cannot be shared. In the case of Lucrece, the 'shame', a word that tolls through the poem like a dismal bell, in no way indicates that she is guilty: rather, it is further proof of the total innocence of her soul, for like Desdemona she takes upon herself the burden of guilt for the sin against her.

Lucrece's shame is a private, self-regarding state which is, of its nature, negative in kind. It is 'unseen', 'invisible', a 'private scar' (827–8). Unlike emotions such as anger, outrage, boredom, joy, frustration and even lust, it cannot be discharged in action, and it cannot be shared with others by speaking about it, because it subverts reason. To an outsider it may appear to be a response completely disproportionate to the cause, and even irrational, but this is to demean the humiliated feelings of the sufferer. She is first seen asleep, and the first violation of her inner world comes when she opens her eyes and sees the treacherous Tarquin, 'The sight which makes supposed terror true' (455). Her trust in appearances is shattered by the new behaviour of her previously courteous guest. After the rape she finds herself smitten with 'helpless shame' (756), locked in the mental torture of spiritual paralysis and grief:

> But I alone alone must sit and pine,
> Seasoning the earth with show'rs of silver brine,
>   Mingling my talk with tears, my grief with groans,
>   Poor wasting monument of lasting moans.
>   (795–8)

Having taken us into the dark mood of Lucrece's mind, Shakespeare allows us to witness her conceptualizing obsessively about her state, as she tries to find a rational answer to her feelings. The body and soul have been torn apart, because before the violent rape they were held together by the fact of fidelity to Collatine, her husband:

> My body or my soul, which was the dearer,
> When the one pure, the other made divine?
> Whose love of either to myself was nearer,
> When both were kept for heaven and Collatine?
>   (1163–6)

Even the syntax mirrors her circling confusion, as she tries to regain the simple sententiousness that could sum up her former life, 'When both were kept for heaven and Collatine'. No atonement, literally 'at-one-ment', between body and soul now seems possible to her, because of the violation of one half of the equation, her body, control over which has been taken away from her. The only defence is to safeguard her soul by punishing the body in suicide:

> The one [the soul] will live, the other being dead.
> So of shame's ashes shall my fame be bred;
>   For in my death I murther shameful scorn.
>   My shame so dead, mine honour is new born.
>   (1187–90)

Suicide is the act which validates her life and the virtue which gave it meaning. When we consider the other victims in Shakespeare, whether or not they actually commit suicide, their state of mind may well be analogous to Lucrece's, although we are not let into the secret of their feelings.

Before the death, however, the narrator discreetly disengages us from the hidden horror of Lucrece's consciousness, in order that we may contemplate her state from a different point of view. He emphasizes the privacy of her self-punishment, its apparent irrationality and incomprehensibility to spectators, by showing her in the company of others. Her degree of distress may be obvious to others, but the cause is a mystery to them, since it lies in a disintegration of the personality, and facts which Lucrece cannot reveal. Lucrece's maid, in silent sympathy shares the frustrated grief of her mistress without understanding it, and the narrator sadly observes, 'To see sad sights moves more than hear them told' (1324). When Lucrece meets the naive groom, he blushes to witness her anguish; she thinks he is seeing into her shameful state; and they both blush all the more, for their different reasons. In these little encounters, Shakespeare takes us away from Lucrece's inward soul and emphasizes the inscrutability of the victim's feelings by demonstrating in social action her inner imprisonment. The rapist has long since gone, unaware of the psychological consequences for his victim, but for the woman they are all too real and terrifying.

By introducing the digression on painting, so typical of the classical *epyllion*,[3] Shakespeare enables us to see the action from yet another point of view, so distant from psychology that we can begin to contemplate the work of art itself, and its relationship with the reality of Lucrece's feelings. Brooding upon the discrepancy between her virtuous appearance and the awareness of shame in her mind, Lucrece looks at some paintings, seeking one that will match and express her own anxiety and grief in its mimetic power. In a sense, the reader of the poem, simply in the act of reading, has been encouraged to regard the work in the same spirit, as an imitation of a character's feelings which, although fictional, become 'real' to the imagination. Lucrece discovers to her surprise that art, at least momentarily, can provide some relief from the burden of time which she must endure in shame before she dies. She begins by inveighing against the tyranny of time, feeling its ruthless persecution:

> Thus ebbs and flows the current of her sorrow,
> And time doth weary time with her complaining.
> She looks for night, and then she longs for morrow,
> And both she thinks too long with her remaining.

Short time seems long in sorrow's sharp sustaining;
  Though woe be heavy, yet it seldom sleeps;
  And they that watch see time how slow it creeps.
    (1569–75)

As she contemplates the images of sorrow in others, however, she finds through the paintings that time is beguiled and defied, and slips by unnoticed:

    Which all this time have overslipp'd her thought
    That she with painted images hath spent,
    Being from the feeling of her own grief brought
    By deep surmise of others detriment,
    Losing her woes in shows of discontent.
      (1576–80)

It is no coincidence that pictorial art, as Keats so whimsically makes clear in his 'Ode on a Grecian Urn', is the one art form that can exclude the tyranny of time, whilst at the same time freezing time so that distress (or joy) will last forever:

    Bold lover, never, never canst thou kiss,
  Though winning near the goal — yet, do not grieve;
    She cannot fade, though thou hast not thy bliss,
    For ever wilt thou love, and she be fair!

Just as an expressive painting may allow Lucrece to contemplate her own feelings from a distance, alleviating the pain by sublimation, so the reader is led by the digression to reflect upon the nature of the poem itself, and its relationship with himself. While we have been reading the poem, we have been encouraged to inhabit imaginatively the mental state of Lucrece, just as she herself becomes implicated in the pictured grief of Hecuba and the malice of Sinon. For the reader, and for Lucrece, the significant detail in a work of art or literature can imply a larger life of feelings and motivations lying 'behind' the canvas of the words, when the imagination is stirred:

    A hand, a foot, a face, a leg, a head,
    Stood for the whole to be imagined.
    (1427–8)

The point is crucial when we examine Shakespeare's innocent

victims in his plays, for one of their common characteristics is an
eloquent silence about their own feelings: Cordelia is only the latest
in a line of characters forced to suffer in silence, and the thoughts of
Lucrece, provided for us in the medium of the narrative poem, help
to explain our imaginative intuitions, 'unseen, save to the eye of
mind' (1426), of the griefs of Lavinia, Ophelia and Desdemona. At
the same time, Lucrece's observations lead us to recognize that the
work of art is set apart from the world of the living, existing in a
static and unchanging dimension:

> She tears the senseless Sinon with her nails,
> Comparing him to that unhappy guest
> Whose deed hath made herself herself detest.
>   At last she smilingly with this gives o'er:
>   'Fool! fool!' quoth she 'his wounds will not be sore.'
>   (1564–8)

The digression about painting shows us that, while we can enter
imaginatively the life of feelings represented in a work of art, we
cannot alter anything in the work. We cannot run on to the stage and
berate Othello for his foolishness in the hope that our action will
change the preordained events of the play. We can, however, as does
Lucrece to some extent, learn from art how to deal with our own
unique situations in the living world so long as we recognize the
separateness. The point is of importance to an understanding of the
whole issue of the educative functions of imaginative literature.

At the end of the poem, as at the beginning, Lucrece is seen only
from the outside. Where she was asleep, now she is dead. She is a
solitary figure, surrounded by buffoons and choleric men, who
regard her rhetoric as hysteria, and even fight against each other
about 'Who should weep most for daughter or for wife' (1792). As
husband and father bicker over the corpse, Collatine crying 'she was
only mine' (1798) and Lucretius claiming 'I owed her' (1803), we
who have been given a glimpse of her feelings recognize that she has
been nobody's but her own, alone with a private struggle waged
between 'herself' and 'herself', her body and her soul, precipitated
by the rape. 'The pale swan in her wat'ry nest' had begun 'the sad
dirge of her certain ending' (1611–12) in solitude, and had killed
herself to maintain the integrity of her soul:

Even here she sheathed in her harmless breast
A harmful knife, that hence her soul unsheathed.
That blow did bail it from the deep unrest
Of that polluted prison where it breathed.
    (1723–6)

'Key-cold Lucrece' bleeding stream' (1774) becomes as much a contemplated object, an artefact, as the painting which had so absorbed her, and she returns to her marmoreal state as a 'virtuous monument', existing now as a myth. In the same way the poem itself, after opening our imaginations to the emotional suffering of the innocent victim, has now closed itself, and become an artefact. Like the paintings seen by Lucrece, it has become a 'sad shadow' of the present, existing now in the stillness of the past, where it has once been a temporal experience.

If it be granted that literature may provide a moral experience as well as an imaginative, what, then, can we find in *The Rape of Lucrece* which will be of use in examining Shakespeare's dramatic innocent victims? The poem proposes two answers to this question, the one less adequate and powerful than the other. The plain, blunt man, Brutus provides one response to the fate of Lucrece, and it is similar to Brecht's advice, 'That you'll go down if you don't stand up for yourself':

'Why, Collatine, is woe the cure for woe?
Do wounds help wounds, or grief help grievous deeds?
. . .

  Thy wretched wife mistook the matter so
  To slay herself that should have slain her foe'.
    (1821–7)

It should be obvious by now that such a comment is both insensitive and unrealistic. Judged against Lucrece's feelings, it does not comprehend the woman's own passivity, solitude and strength of self-regard, all qualities which are congenital to her, as to the other victims in Shakespeare. It is no use telling a person to turn suffering into anger and action, when the suffering itself rejects the notion of the violence which caused the situation. Again, killing the foe might be a realistic option for a man, at least in Roman society, but hardly for a woman. It cannot eradicate the initial male violence either, and in fact physical violence, as in *Titus Andronicus*, would simply reinforce the ethic of hatred. It is neither within the personality nor the capabilities of Lucrèce to act as Brutus would have a woman act in such circumstances.

The narrator provides us with another 'moral' which directs our attention to the social disease of violent domination exemplified by Tarquin's rape. In a rare aside which is one of the few occasions when the narrator makes an overt comment rather than allowing the story and the characters to speak for themselves, he lays the blame squarely upon the society for the tragedy which has occurred:

> The weak oppress'd, th'impression of strange kinds
> Is form'd in them by force, by fraud, or skill.
> Then call them not the authors of their ill,
>   No more than wax shall be accounted evil
>   Wherein is stamp'd the semblance of a devil.
>   (1242–6)

Despite its quietly rueful tone, there is an intensity of social criticism behind the comment. In an ideal society where the strong do not oppress the weak by means of force, fraud or skill, there would be no rape and consequently no mental anguish comparable to Lucrece's shame.

The next comment is even more explicit:

> No man inveigh against the withered flow'r
> But chide rough winter that the flow'r hath kill'd.
> Not that devour'd but that which doth devour,
> Is worthy blame. Oh, let it not be hild
> Poor women's faults that they are so fulfill'd
>   With men's abuses! those proud lords to blame
>   Make weak-made women tenants to their shame.
>   (1254–60)

Such statements provide a moral framework within which we may interpret the action. Without them, the reader would have to draw the conclusion for himself, as one must in a play, where there is no trustworthy narrator. In the poem and the plays alike, Shakespeare is not simply being 'chameleon-like', delighting in virtue and vice equally, for the whole design is held in close moral check. Constantly, as we shall see in the context of the drama, we in the audience must be alert to our own moral sympathies which are aroused and guided by the dramatist. We should be on our guard against being deceived and decoyed by the skilled rhetoric of the people of 'force' in plays, for to succumb would be to deny the moral design in which the existence of innocent victims is of crucial importance.

Because this section has been designed to lead on to a discussion of Shakespeare's victims in his tragedies, I have consciously emphasized one aspect of the poem's design at the expense of discussion of its mode. *The Rape of Lucrece* is the one work which perhaps betrays Shakespeare working beyond his own scope of understanding. Admittedly, the poem is sometimes artificially rhetorical, there are moments of inappropriate irony, and to speak of psychological penetration has an anachronistic flavour. None the less, it is important to respect the intention of the work as a narrative description of the feelings of a character in deep distress, written at a time when, apart from Sidney's *Arcadia*, there was little precedent on such a sustained scale in English. Attempts to read the poem in a systematically ironic light should now have been discredited by a recent critic, Richard Levin[4] who, using external evidence, shows that there was no supporting authority for an ironically presented Lucrece. Somewhat laboured the poem may be, awkward in details of tone and revealing subtle areas of incomprehension in the writer's imaginative grasp of a woman's experience of rape, but the overwhelming evidence is that he took that experience more seriously than anybody else who had, until his time, dealt with the myth, that he subordinates sensation to reflection, and that he displays the kind of fundamental concern for the victim which we shall see repeated in his plays.[5] It is not until Richardson writes *Clarissa* in the eighteenth century that we even find an attempt made at such a delicate and daunting task.

V Children

At least since the time of Christ, the child has been taken to be the symbol of absolute innocence. When an adult is the victim, somebody can always raise the possibility that the person has collaborated in the outcome by acts of personal responsibility. Desdemona is said to be a liar, Ophelia too pliable, Lucrece masochistic, Cordelia unco-operative. Although in answer to these charges we may consistently argue that the victim is caught in a web of circumstances which diminishes individual control, yet at least we must recognize the existence of a possible disagreement. No such problem occurs when the victim is a child, for we presume innocence and incorruptibility. If a child is killed in a work of literature, the writer is invariably laying the blame at the feet of some malevolent person, or a guilty society.

Not accidentally, the occasions on which Shakespeare presents the violation of a child's defenceless vulnerability are predominantly political plays, and our moral sympathies are stirred not only against individual rulers such as Richard III, Macbeth or King John, but also against the political society and attitudes which they represent. These plays also give us more evidence that the predominant critical approach which builds an argument about the internal suffering of the great man, is not only untrue to a total impression of the play in the theatre or on the page, but is also dangerously close to being immoral. If we concentrate upon the mental states of Macbeth, Richard III and King John, we are able to find plenty of self-justifying statements from each to suggest that they are pawns of fortune, rather than worldly figures of authority and power in the state, with a consequent responsibility to exercise their power with ethical propriety. To put the matter a different way, if we judge Shylock by his feelings, we may easily apologize for his murderous designs on the life of Antonio in *The Merchant of Venice*. On the other hand, if we judge him primarily by his actions, we may more properly place his psychological make-up as a product of social and political pressures, without going to the extent of condoning his attempted murder. The heroes in the tragedies and especially the three rulers who appear in this chapter may be assessed in a similar way. No matter how imaginatively impressionable is Macbeth, no matter how embittered is Richard against the ostracizing qualities of society, and no matter how lonely is John, they are all, strictly speaking, cold-blooded and ruthless murderers for political ends. If we seek to find some ultimate reason for the existence of evil amongst men, and if we also do not wish to ignore the fact that each villain is partially a victim of circumstances himself, then the next step is to look at the society itself which perpetuates myths of the moral licence given to powerful men. Those men remain, none the less, as symptoms of the general disease. The method the plays use to encourage such a morally attuned attitude, is to give us some victims who are children, so that the point cannot be missed. At the same time, we must quickly qualify this statement when we come to examine particular examples. With his shrewdness of insight into human behaviour, Shakespeare also gives us the disturbing sight of the child's innocence, itself at the threshold of an insidious corruption, precociously acquiring an adult's political acumen. The lesson of public corruption is enforced all the more potently when we watch a subtle undermining of innocence which occurs even before the shocking fact of assassination. *Richard III* and *Macbeth* show us children only briefly, although there is telling significance in each appearance. We shall merely glance at them with appropriate brevity. In *King John*, however, the boy Arthur is fully characterized and his presence is important to the design of the play in a more systematic way. For this reason, and because the play itself is perhaps in more need of reassessment than the other two, we shall examine him in more detail.

Although Richard before and after he attains the crown is personally guilty of a veritable massacre of the innocents, killing several children and adults as he climbs through briars towards the throne, two significant facts demonstrate that he is the product of an already corrupted political system. First, he personally believes himself to be a victim of social attitudes. Faced with the physical loathing and contempt of the powerful people around, he sees no reason to be scrupulous about imitating their own tactics to win power, with the only difference that he must stand alone, without the support of a faction. Secondly, as Richard gloatingly points out, it was not he who initiated either the struggle for power or the murderous strategies. He turns on the old queen, Margaret:

> *Gloucester*: The curse my noble father laid on thee,
>   When thou didst crown his warlike brows with paper
>   And with thy scorns drew'st rivers from his eyes,
>   And then to dry them gav'st the Duke a clout
>   Steep'd in the faultless blood of pretty Rutland —
>   His curses then from bitterness of soul
>   Denounc'd against thee are all fall'n upon thee;
>   And God, not we, hath plagu'd thy bloody deed.
> *Queen Elizabeth*: So just is God to right the innocent.
> *Hastings*: O, 'twas the foulest deed to slay that babe,
>   And the most merciless that e'er was heard of!
> *Rivers*: Tyrants themselves wept when it was reported.
> *Dorset*: No man but prophesied revenge for it.
> *Buckingham*: Northumberland, then present, wept to see it.
>   (I.iii.174–87)

Margaret points out the obvious irony of the situation, allowing us
to see clearly that in this society nobody has a spotless conscience:

> What, were you snarling all before I came,
> Ready to catch each other by the throat,
> And turn you all your hatred now on me?
>   (I.iii.188–90)

She goes on to accuse each of her persecutors of the same unprincipled cruelty when they were onlookers to the assassination of her
own son, who died 'in his youth by like untimely violence'
(I.iii.201). It is crucial that at the beginning of this play of political
ambition and unprincipled murder, we are forced to recognize that
nobody is innocent, and the reported fate of children allows us to see
this. The outrage expressed by any one character must always be
interpreted in a harsh light, for it is clear that virtually all the
characters would be prepared to murder, if it would allow them to
achieve, or retain, power in the state.

    Shakespeare evokes little true pity in this play, for it would
interfere with the anger. Even the children themselves are not fully
invested with the lamb-like qualities that would stir our pathos, for
the two main victims, the Prince of Wales and the Duke of York,
although youthful and innocent, are given moments that display a

budding capacity for political circumspection: 'So cunning and so young is wonderful' (III.f.135). The circumstances of one death that allows us to register consciously what is happening is the murder of the adult, Clarence, in the Tower. One of his assassins has 'some certain dregs of conscience' yet within him, but he temporarily acquiesces when reminded of the reward, a poor man's equivalent of political power which, in the world of this play, will drive men to murder:

> 1 *Murderer*: Remember our reward, when the deed's done.
> 2 *Murderer*: Zounds, he dies; I had forgot the reward.
> 1 *Murderer*: Where's thy conscience now?
> 2 *Murderer*: O, in the Duke of Gloucester's purse!
> 1 *Murderer*: When he opens his purse to give us our reward, thy conscience flies out.
> 2 *Murderer*: 'Tis no matter, let it go; there's few or none will entertain it.
> (I.iv.123–31)

He goes on to rationalize away the dictates of the conscience as being the blandishment of the devil. After the deed he has another moment of shame:

> A bloody deed, and desperately dispatch'd!
> How fain, like Pilate, would I wash my hands
> Of this most grievous murder!
> (I.iv.269–71)

The reference to Pilate is interesting. In a play in which many characters call upon God or use Christian imagery in order to justify acts of self-seeking brutality, the reader or audience may find himself in the position of Pilate, seeing through manifest injustices and yet powerless to find a principle of true justice portrayed in action. The eventual death of Richard has both poetic and divine justice, but we are left with the nasty suspicion that the root causes of corruption, kingship and power, are still stalking the country.

Macbeth is a play centrally concerned with the psychology and consequences of political ambition and power. It is difficult for us to stand back from the internal tumult of Macbeth himself during the first half of the play, for it gives us little opportunity to judge the central character from the outside, so compellingly is his own mental state presented, in a sweep of concentrated attention and soliloquy. Soon after the death of Duncan however, the protagonist disappears from our view, we have time to breathe and to contemplate the significance of his actions. When he reappears, the imaginative richness and tension has gone from his language, and he struggles on, wavering between desolate emptiness and manic bravado, a morally empty being. In the scheme of the play, the little scene in which Macduff's son is killed by anonymous murderers has a clear and important function, allowing us to examine the moral impropriety of Macbeth's actions in unleashing the consequences of political assassination in the state.

The tyrant's actions have led the virtuous Macduff to desert his wife and family, in fact for political reasons, a betrayal which glares the more seriously to his wife than does his betrayal of Macbeth. The scene is partly a reproach to the father as much as to the king, and it is disturbing that the child himself is already learning the way of such a world:

> Then the liars and swearers are fools; for there are liars and
> swearers enow to beat the honest men and hang them up.
> (IV.ii.55–7)

The main point of the scene, however, is not the corruption of youth but the destruction of it. After giving us a glimpse of domesticity and family anxiety, Shakespeare snatches away the child in a moment as brief as it is brutal, when hired assassins abruptly stab him. Supporting the political function of the scene, the imagery has significance. Throughout the play there is constant reference to birds, which are mainly predatory: raven, owl, falcon, bat, hawk, 'maggot-pies, and choughs, and rooks' (III.iv.125). There has been an early glimpse of the domestic bird, the temple-haunting martlet, who makes his 'pendent bed and procreant cradle' (I.vi.8) around the dwellings of men. The reference to the harmless bird of summer, before the death of Duncan, is like a window opening out of a dark room, reminding us of burgeoning nature, temples, and the delicate air. In the remainder of the play, the birds of prey take malevolent control. In the scene showing the stabbing of the boy, Shakespeare reminds us of the plight of the smaller birds which nest in vulnerable places. Macduff's wife likens herself to such birds:

for the poor wren,
The most diminutive of birds, will fight,
Her young ones in the nest, against the owl.
    (IV.ii.9–11)

Macduff later sees the event in terms of his 'pretty chickens' killed by a 'hell-kite' (IV.iii.216–18). The shocking unnaturalness of a species preying upon itself, the falcon hawked at by the mousing owl (II.iv.12–13), is emphasized by the likening of the boy to the 'poor birds' that feed on worms and flies, fearing neither the net nor lime, only to be rapidly killed by a fellow human being. With the murderer's words as he stabs, 'What, you egg?' (IV.ii.84) we find the most grotesque example of the consequences of Macbeth's actions: predators feeding on their own embryos. It would be reassuring to think that Macbeth's eventual death will heal the state, but as Malcolm realizes in a horrifying glimpse of his own dark nature in the next scene, 'the imperial charge' of power itself will change even the most virtuous nature. The scene of the boy's killing is designed to stir feelings not of pathos, but of horror and anger. It stands as an emblem for the others who are murdered, Duncan and Banquo, and it stirs the operation of our 'pity, like a naked, new-born babe' all the more immediately because the victim here is himself a child. The scene marks the part of the play in which our stunned feelings begin to awaken from a rapt contemplation of the actions of Macbeth, heralding a moral awareness of their nature. Without the scene, the check upon our imaginative endorsement of Macbeth's compulsive ambition would be diminished, we should see the man more as victim than as murderer, and the play would be open to charges of uncritical sadism. However horrifying is the murder of the boy, its function is to bring us back to our moral senses.[1]

In its own way, *King John* is the most cynical play Shakespeare ever wrote. The death of the child, Arthur, is received with so many self-interested reactions from the characters, that we trust any one response at our peril, and we are given little vocal justification for any caring response at all. However, there is just enough for us legitimately to hold a powerful sense of outrage that must condemn the nobles at their sport, so intent upon their own quest for power that they lose sight of a young life snatched away. Shakespeare leaves it *almost* all up to us to draw conclusions about this death, for little rhetoric is spared on its significance.

Although *King John* is a tragedy in form, there is a vein of humour running through the play. It involves irony of a particular, cruel kind, appreciated by the audience but not often by characters. Throughout, we recognize the ironies in the unscrupulously expedient changes of plan adopted by the rival kings, as they rationalize first one policy, then another, with equal fervour. This is particularly evident in the long scene before the walls of Angiers (II.i), as John, Philip, and the King of Austria, in opposition to each other, alternately cajole, trade with, and threaten the townspeople to yield up the city, whilst the Citizen, acting like a coy lady from courtly love tradition before two lovers, suggests that the kings should fight out the issue of power:

> Till you compound whose right is worthiest,
> We for the worthiest hold the right from both.
> (II.i.281–2)

In petulant frustration, to the dismay of the town, the kings defeat their own purposes by accepting the suggestion that they should join forces to destroy the obstinately recalcitrant (i.e. innocently helpless) town:

Bastard: An if thou hast the mettle of a king,
> Being wrong'd as we are by this peevish town,
> Turn thou the mouth of thy artillery,
> As we will ours, against these saucy walls;
> And when that we have dash'd them to the ground,
> Why then defy each other, and pell-mell
> Make work upon ourselves, for heaven and hell.
King Philip: Let it be so. Say, where will you assault?
King John: We from the west will send destruction
> Into this city's bosom.
Austria: I from the north.
King Philip: Our thunder from the south,
> Shall rain their drift of bullets on this town.
> (II.i.401–13)

The mischievously detached Bastard, far more intelligent than anybody else in the play, and cynically aware of the stupidity of political logic, has been fanning the fire of conflict mainly for his own amusement:

> [*Aside*] O prudent discipline! From north to south,
> Austria and France shoot in each other's mouth.
> I'll stir them to it . . .
> (II.i.413–14)

(From this point in our history, it is impossible not to apply to contemporary situations the analogy of 'superpowers' fighting each other in undeveloped countries, at the cost of the destruction of innocent territory.) The reaction of the Citizen, in sudden alarm, is to suggest a new compromise, an arranged marriage between England and France, and the kings instantly accept the proposal. The humour comes from a very simple source, our recognition that there are so many kings, apparently opposing each other yet indistinguishable in their reasoning powers. The confrontation takes on an irresistible similarity to Tweedledum and Tweedledee, and the jauntiness of the Bastard allows us a mouthpiece for this point of view:

> Mad worlds! mad kings! mad composition!
> (II.i.561)

and he unerringly puts his finger on the cause:

> Commodity, the bias of the world,
> The world, who of itself is peised well,
> Made to run even upon even ground,
> Till this advantage, this vile-drawing bias,
> This sway of motion, this commodity,
> Makes it head for all indifferency,
> From all direction, purpose, course, intent —
> . . .
> (II.i.574–80)

Scathing and sardonic, his analysis is in the key of Sir Thomas More's disgust at the primacy of economic priorities, voiced in *Utopia*.[2] The Bastard goes on:

> Well, whiles I am a beggar, I will rail.
> And say there is no sin but to be rich;

> And being rich, my virtue then shall be
> To say there is no vice but beggary.
>   (II.i.593–6)

The humour in the scene, then, derives from the mercenary self-interest of the kings, in unashamedly making economic concerns of power the centre of their morality and the justification for their actions. Except in the Bastard, there is no respect for individuality, and there is no 'direction, purpose, course, intent'.

Such a sceptical tone is sustained in most of the play. Constance, for example, although apparently nobly concerned for the welfare of England in pressing her claims for the child Arthur's rights to the Crown, and grief-stricken when he has been abducted, has never fully convinced readers of her sincerity. Her ambitions for the helpless boy are too nakedly political and self-seeking, and her grief, in consequence, sounds too close to histrionic self-pity to strike us as a genuine concern for the child's welfare. Admittedly, Mrs Siddons could apparently give grandeur to the part, and 'bring out the tenderness of Constance's love for Arthur',[3] but somehow such a theatrical feat may be achieved only by tapping conventional respect for the 'suffering within' of the mentally agonized, eloquent, tragic protagonist. True pity, as we shall see, lies in a perception of the silent spectacle of the child himself, rather than in the mother's wails:

> Therefore never, never
> Must I behold my pretty Arthur more.
> *Randulph*: You hold too heinous a respect of grief.
> *Constance*: He talks to me that never had a son.
> *King Philip*: You are as fond of grief as of your child.
>   (III.iv.88–92)

The overt callousness of the men is at least partly matched, when we look at the sequence of events, by the self-interest of a mother who has virtually caused the fate of her child by pushing him, reluctantly and in all his inexperience, into the world of politics, in order to fulfil her own ambitions.

The suspicion that in the world of this play people are being used like pawns in a political chess game hinges on the presence of Arthur, and it is his plight which draws out the only true feelings expressed in the play. As in his presentation of children in other plays,

Shakespeare attaches to Arthur a set of images that confirm his position as innocent victim:

> By my christendom,
> So I were out of prison and kept sheep,
> I should be as merry as the day is long.
> (iv.i.16–18)

> Nay, hear me, Hubert! Drive these men away,
> And I will sit as quiet as a lamb;
> . . .
> (iv.i.79–80)

There is much talk of lions elsewhere, an image applied to high-born and courageous men. In a different context, the 'lions' could arouse admiration, but juxtaposed with the true lamb, they reveal themselves as braggarts, self-seekers, and bullies. Again, even Arthur himself becomes embarrassed and faintly puzzled by his mother's hysteria:

> Good my mother, peace!
> I would that I were low laid in my grave.
> I am not worth this coil that's made for me.
> (ii.i.163–5)

Ironically, he is too naively honest to understand that the question of true 'worth' as a person is not being considered by anybody. His value for others is that of a 'commodity', a tool for the power-seeking. Arthur stands throughout 'with a powerless hand' (ii.i.15), unable to avoid the cold exploitations into which he is thrust. His cry is pathetically apt to the situation in which political goals are considered over and above human qualities: 'Is it my fault that I was Geffrey's son?' (iv.i.22). Shakespeare's presentation allows us to distance ourselves from the other characters, and to see their malice as inadvertently comic, and therefore all the more dangerous, in its mechanistic ruthlessness. He does this by placing at the centre a recognizably vulnerable, innocent child.

The danger of such a strategy for the dramatist, is that the audience, by having to do the work of interpretation, might miss the point that is being made about the outrageousness of injustice in a political context. Without some more explicit demonstration, the audience, however morally intelligent, might even be tempted to think the dramatist himself approves of political expedience as a course of action, and is simply exploiting the boy for his own purposes. The play would then be very cynical indeed, dismissing conscience as stupidly ineffectual, experience as unremittingly malicious, and leaving only the most devious, machiavellian politicians at the centre. In order to counter the dangers, Shakespeare places at the heart of the play a scene in which Hubert, commissioned to assassinate Arthur, is stirred to a compassion which the audience must respect and share. One recent commentator, perhaps a little reluctant in the modern way to confess the effectiveness of broad pathos, finds in this scene a way of explaining the operation of our pity in a complex way. He suggests that Arthur demonstrates a kind of cunning in trying to manipulate Hubert's responses by employing a calculated rhetoric: 'His conceits do not ring prettily because "innocent prate" (IV.i.25) when turned "crafty" and "cunning" (IV.i.53–4), like beauty selling itself, distorts and defaces itself.'[4] The analysis continues: 'Not his terror, but the sight of a child forced into duplicity, produces the more subtle pathos of the scene.' Although undoubtedly the point is sensitively made, and it is consistent with the hint of political precocity which Shakespeare gives the other children in these plays, yet it is necessary to stress the primary pathos as well as the 'more subtle'. We could put the matter differently by saying that the child's rhetoric should be seen as the dramatist's calculation to raise the audience's feelings, rather than evidence of deviousness in the child. The broadest emotional effect raised is a pity and terror at the sight of the boy's vulnerability in the face of his executioners, and the terrifyingly visual threat to his soft eyes of the hot iron rods. What happens in the scene is not that Hubert is persuaded by the calculated conceits of a child with the budding skill of a politician. Hubert is emotionally convinced by feelings he finds in himself, irrespective of the child's language. He suddenly recognizes, in a moment which asserts the power of the feelings and the conscience, that he is engaged in an appalling and unforgivable act of cruelty. He sees that the humanity of the 'pretty child' is an infinitely higher value than any 'commodity', and unfortunately he himself comes to suffer for his moment of moral lucidity:

> Well, see to live; I will not touch thine eye
> For all the treasure that thine uncle owes.
>   (IV..i.122–3)

If Rilke was right in saying that the final defence is defencelessness, then this scene presents us with a good proof.

The death of Arthur is, at least in its immediate causes, an accident, and Shakespeare presents it with such brevity that we are not allowed much time for pity. He tries to escape from the castle, dressed as a sailor-boy, and is killed in the jump from the walls, uttering the words, 'As good to die and go, as die and stay . . .' (IV.iii.8). Isolated, exploited and hounded during his short life, his final statement amounts to a suicidal intention, although one cannot avoid feeling that he has been murdered by the forces which have been victimizing him. From this point onwards, the focus is upon the responses which his death provokes from others, and upon the political consequences. There are three significant results: the continuation of the political machinations by the enemies of John; a new alliance between the only two characters in the play who have feelings and a conscience, Hubert and the Bastard; and the emotional consequences for John himself. We shall look at each in turn.

In death, as in life, Arthur is treated as a 'commodity' by the politicians. When Hubert falsely reports the death, Salisbury and Pembroke sternly reproach John for 'apparent foul play', and although their indignation is severe and justified, there comes a point where Pembroke hints that the political consequences will prove more troublesome than any amount of moral heart-searching:

> . . . bad world the while!
> This must not be borne: this will break out
> To all our sorrows, and ere long I doubt.
>   (IV.ii.100–3)

His guess proves correct, for almost immediately the Bastard enters to report mounting opposition to John:

> Besides, I met Lord Bigot and Lord Salisbury,
> With eyes as red as new-kindled fire,
> And others more, going to seek the grave
> Of Arthur, whom they say is kill'd tonight
> On your suggestion.
>   (IV.ii.162–6)

The plot on Arthur's life is regretted not because it was unjust, but
because it was politically inexpedient. John's opposition is quick to
exploit the mistake. Hubert brings reports of unrest and fear
amongst the common people as the rumours spread that the French
are arriving and that Arthur is dead:

> Another lean, unwash'd artificer
> Cuts off his tale and talks of Arthur's death.
>   (iv.ii.201–2)

At this point, ironically, Arthur is not dead, but he is by the time the
lords arrive on the scene. Even before they find the body, they are
determined to believe rumours which so much discredit John. As the
lords seek to disassociate themselves from John, the intensity of their
accusations contrasts markedly with the Bastard's restraint, and it is
clear that their prime motives are to find a scapegoat and to leave a
failing king as expeditiously as possible:

> *Salisbury*: The king hath dispossess'd himself of us.
>   We will not line his thin bestained cloak
>   With our pure honours, nor attend the foot
>   That leaves the print of blood where'er it walks.
>   Return and tell him so. We know the worst.
> *Bastard*: Whate'er you think, good words, I think, were best.
> *Salisbury*: Our griefs, and not our manners, reason now.
> *Bastard*: But there is little reason in your grief;
>   Therefore, 'twere reason you had manners now.
> *Pembroke*: Sir, sir, impatience hath his privilege.
> *Bastard*: 'Tis true — to hurt his master, no man else.
>   (iv.iii.23–33)

The first thought in the minds of the lords is 'revenge', which really
seems to be an excuse for a calculated political realignment of their
support. As Hubert enters, they forget any decorum springing from
'grief', and instead they threaten him with death. The 'morsel of
dead royalty' (iv.iii.143) lies neglected in the heat of violent accusations and haughty self-defence. The scene recalls the death of
Lucrece.

The Bastard, who has already attracted our sympathy by his
jaunty bravado, by the shrewdly penetrating accuracy of his perceptions, and above all by his consistent appeals to 'fair-play' (v.ii.118),

acts according to 'reason', and seriously interrogates Hubert in order to learn the truth. As R.L. Smallwood points out, since the audience knows the truth, we are grateful that somebody in the play is so intent upon fair adjudication.[5] Because Hubert has already placed his personal feelings and conscience above narrowly political considerations, there is a new-found trust between himself and the Bastard, which at last provides a serious, moral equilibrium within the play, justifying and reaffirming our earlier intuition concerning the callous opportunism of the other characters. Both are now sadder and more serious. The Bastard is given another choric soliloquy, and this time his tone is not the amused dismissiveness of 'Mad world! mad kings!' but a more involved anxiety:

> Now, for the bare-pick'd bone of majesty
> Doth dogged war bristle his angry crest
> And snarleth in the gentle eyes of peace
>
> . . .
>
> (IV.iii.148–50)

Throughout, his responses show a deeply felt moral discrimination between personal values and political. In his actions he is also consistently loyal. Although recognizing the invalid quality of John's course of action, and acknowledging the truth of Arthur's claim to the throne, he never abandons his own allegiance to the king. He has acquired the authority and commitment to humane values to enable him to turn upon the other characters and accuse them all of causing the death of Arthur, who by this time stands for England:

> And you degenerate, you ingrate revolts,
> You bloody Neroes, ripping up the womb
> Of your dear mother England, blush for shame;
>
> . . .
>
> (v.ii.151–3)

To the audience, the statement comes as a truth, and holds the power of conviction, but the other characters are still too self-absorbed and self-interested to listen to 'such a brabbler' (v.ii.162). Meanwhile, the other character of conscience, Hubert, is seen as a sad and lonely man, wandering in the black brow of night to find the only man who has trusted or believed him (v.vi.).

For King John himself, the consequences of Arthur's death are disastrous. At first, like the lords, he responds to the news political-ly, unfairly berating Hubert for not resisting his command to kill Arthur, and thinking of means to avert the political repercussions: 'I have a way to win their loves again' (IV.ii.168). He is much more personally moved and upset by the news of his mother's death. Even his first 'repentance' is couched not in terms of conscience, but of the inexpedience of assassination:

> They burn in indignation. I repent.
> There is no sure foundation set on blood,
> No certain life achiev'd by others' death
>   (IV.ii.103–5)

The true indifference to the sanctity of individual human life lying behind this statement is proved by his easy modulation into optimis-tic enthusiasm when Hubert confides that the boy is not dead. The former intention to kill is completely forgotten in the desire to make new strategies which will not arouse such opposition. John has learned a political lesson (too late), but in real terms he is consider-ably less wise than his own hired assassin.

To the very end, John resists making any admission of guilt in human terms, and his thoughts tend towards the 'suffering within' of the self-proclaimed tragic protagonist. He speaks of his 'unre-prievable condemned blood', but his final speeches reveal not shame but an awareness of moral emptiness, and a reproachful sense of the ingratitude of those who will not give even 'cold comfort' (v.ii.43) in his dying moments. This should not strike him as particularly surprising, in view of the fact that he has unrelentingly involved himself in the very political machinery which is now crushing him. Poisoned in body, his strange fantasies and astonishing images reflect a spiritual poison and vacuity which he cannot locate:

> I am a scribbled form drawn with a pen
> Upon a parchment, and against this fire
> Do I shrink up.
>   (v.vii.32–4)

> The tackle of my heart is crack'd and burnt,
> And all the shrouds wherewith my life should sail

Are turned to one thread, one little hair;
My heart hath one poor string to stay it by,

. . .

(v.vii.52–5)

The empty value-system sustained by John in his political role now turns into a dreadful agent of self-persecution. He judges himself as he has judged others, as objects, commodities and ciphers, and finds nothing to live for.

The causes and consequences of Arthur's death in *King John* are not presented as if they have any kind of 'poetic justice'. In the play, the guilty are left unrepentant, the *status quo* is maintained, even after John's death. Political objectives, never including a notion of the sanctity of human life, inexorably take revenge over individuals, but the moral order does not change. Those involved in the political system in a position of power have never realized their transgression of a moral law, so it cannot properly be said that John's death is a symbolic punishment in the sense that the suicides of Othello or Enobarbus can be. However, with the privilege of distance, there is an irresistible undertow of moral doctrine, given a touching moment of human feeling in Hubert's mercy, given a vehemently outraged voice through the Bastard, and given a pitiable emblem in the corpse of the child Arthur, treated in life and in death as a mere political commodity. Much of the lesson, however, must come from our own consciences, for if we do not find our outrage awakened by manifest injustice, we risk being as malevolent (or as confused) as those characters in the play who hold political office, and who find it more convenient to follow political logic rather than the moral imagination.

VI Ophelia

Hamlet is a play full of victims, some more innocent than others. The hero himself does little to create the situation that confronts him, and there are at least two plots to assassinate him instigated by Claudius. Once he decides upon a clear line of action, however, Hamlet accepts the violent norms of his adversary, and becomes personally responsible for several deaths. His history shows something about the court of Elsinore, a place where political machinations, eavesdropping, spying, state secrecy and calculated lying create an atmosphere of mutual mistrust and brutal counter-measures so strong that even a representative of forces of good becomes fundamentally tainted. Besides, Hamlet has a luxury normally denied to Shakespeare's victims, a status which allows him to expect that his story will become well known, in a way which might lead to a measure of change in the attitudes of others:

> O God! Horatio, what a wounded name,
> Things standing thus unknown, shall live behind me!
> If thou didst ever hold me in thy heart,
> Absent thee from felicity awhile,
> And in this harsh world draw thy breath in pain,
> To tell my story.
>   (v.ii.336–41)

By the end of the play he is neither innocent nor anonymous. Polonius, Gertrude, Laertes, Rosencrantz and Guildenstern die through no direct fault of their own, but they have all to some extent colluded in the machinery of a rotten state. Polonius has been the crafty politician throughout, never questioning his orders from above, and simply doing his job. Laertes, despite his one moment of 'conscience' (v.ii.288), allows himself to be manipulated by Claudius, and he accepts the violent path of the revenge ethic even without the scruples held by Hamlet. Rosencrantz and Guildenstern, also obeying orders, find themselves in the role of hired assassins. Gertrude is perhaps the most pitiable of all, for her error was almost perpetrated in ignorance. She was simply pliable to the easy way of accepting reassurance and the promise of security from a protective, patriarchal figure. However gullible, she has been implicated in the web of evil spun by the King. There is complete poetic justice in the death of Claudius, and at least qualified fairness in the deaths of the others who have, one way or another, accepted a prevailing morality of violence, coercion and political corruption.

Ophelia's death is much more difficult to come to terms with, and if tragedy were defined as an outrageously unjustified death, then the play should be re-named 'The Tragedy of Ophelia'. She is a true victim, allowed to suffer by an uncaring and cynical world, until she melts away into a death which is condemned even by the church as suicide. In order to understand more clearly what is 'rotten' in the state of Denmark, a fact which the other characters cover up and refuse to acknowledge, we should pay close attention to Ophelia's plight.

The impression of Ophelia most people carry from the play is that of wistful pathos. Her character is marked by an incompleteness which tempts critics to add some dimension, ranging from inexperienced demureness to the physical condition of pregnancy and the depravity of one who 'was not a chaste young woman'.[1] Inside the play characters appear to foist upon Ophelia interpretations for which there seems little evidence in her behaviour.[2] Laertes and Polonius regard her as having the gullibility to succumb easily to Hamlet's blandishments, and they impute the same susceptibility in her to physical desire which they want to find in Hamlet:

> Ay, springs to catch woodcocks! I do know,
> When the blood burns, how prodigal the soul
> Lends the tongue vows.
> (I.iii.115–7)

Hamlet himself in the nunnery scene is ready to see in Ophelia all the hypocritical wiles of the harlot, and even such a sensitive reader of Shakespeare as John Keats likens his own view of Fanny Brawne to Hamlet's of Ophelia:

> If my health would bear it, I could write a Poem which I have in my head, which would be a consolation for people in such a situation as mine. I would show someone in Love as I am, with a person living in Liberty as you do. Shakespeare always sums up

matters in the most sovereign manner. Hamlet's heart was full of such Misery as mine is when he said to Ophelia 'Go to a Nunnery go, go!' Indeed I should like to give up the matter at once — I should like to die.[3]

It is distressing to find Hamlet's disordered vision of Ophelia invoked with such vehemence to justify a dubious attitude.

We do better to ignore the distortions of critics and characters and to concentrate upon the very incompleteness in Ophelia's personality, the readiness for filling one of these roles rather than any particular role. Ophelia is tantalizingly insufficient because of her immaturity. To be more precise, since her main preoccupation during the play is her relationship with Hamlet and its consequences, her immaturity may be defined in terms of the blighting of this relationship. She is innocent, on the brink of sexual commitment, simultaneously fearing and desiring a full love relationship with Hamlet, and trapped by circumstances outside her control. Lawrence's poem, 'Ballad of Another Ophelia', catches the tone of her failure :

> Nothing now will ripen the bright green apples,
> Full of disappointment and of rain.

His line 'What, then is peeping there hidden in the skirts of all the blossom?' and its answer 'Yea, but it is cruel when undressed in all the blossom' gather the distress and pathos of Ophelia's complicated feelings about sexual love. In fact, many artists and poets have found in Ophelia an image of unfulfilled, wasted innocence, from the jewelled surface of Millais' famous painting of the drowning woman, to Walter de la Mare's words:

> There runs a criss cross pattern of small leaves
> Espalier, in a fading summer air,
> And there Ophelia walks, an azure flower,
> Whom wind, and snowflakes, and the sudden rain
> Of love's wild skies have purified to heaven.
> There is a beauty past all weeping now
> In that sweet, crooked mouth, that vacant smile;
> Only a lonely grey in those mad eyes,
> Which never on earth shall learn their loneliness.
>
> . . .

And lest, at last, the world should learn half-secrets;
Lest that sweet wolf from some dim thicket steal;
Better the glassy horror of the stream.
　　　('Ophelia')

What, then, does go wrong with the relationship? Hamlet and Ophelia are ideal candidates for a romantic comedy. They are both in the 'morn and liquid dew of youth', he intelligent and witty enough to be a Benedick, she a graceful and reticent 'rose of May'. He has wooed her ardently and in honourable fashion with almost all the holy vows of heaven. His love-song (ii.ii.114–8) betrays no deception or indecency, and his declaration of love is as sincere and callow as that of any Shakespearean lover:

> O dear Ophelia, I am ill at these numbers. I have not art to reckon my groans; but that I love thee best, O most best believe it. Adieu.
> 　　　(ii.ii.119–21)

His last words on the matter, beside her grave, are 'I lov'd Ophelia' and his mother laments there, 'I hop'd thou shouldst have been my Hamlet's wife' (v.i.238). It is not enough to point to *Romeo and Juliet* and *Othello* and say that there may be tragedies of love as well as comedies. This is to lower both comedy and tragedy to the level of conventional expectations, and to deny them the possibility of common access to psychological truth. There is nothing in the love itself to sow its own destruction, and there is little to link Ophelia with the truly destructive situation, the murder of old Hamlet and the hasty remarriage of his wife. The parental opposition of Polonius, far from being an impediment, would in a comedy be an invigorating challenge for lovers, and he encourages little more respect than the waspish Egeus in *A Midsummer Night's Dream*. Why, then, is Ophelia, 'the young, the beautiful, the harmless and the pious',[4] sacrificed so unjustly?

One formalistic answer is that Ophelia commits a sin against the laws that would apply in a comedy. Instead of allowing her eyes and heart to teach her what she must do, she listens to advice from her brother and father. Like Hamlet, she falls victim to the difficulty of determining how far 'seeming' is being. Even though she has received only honourable courtship from Hamlet, the badgering of Laertes and Polonius in their separate ways is so consistent, emphasizing alike Hamlet's youth and the fiery, mercurial nature of sexual desire, that she is confused. 'I do not know, my lord, what I should think' (I.iii.104) shows distressed docility and fear, pleading for tuition from an experienced elder. The advice she receives is 'Do not believe his vows'. The irony is that her own subsequent conduct seems to Hamlet, who is probably just as innocent as she, a calculated fraud which helps to shatter his own faith in appearances. Her timid words to him later reveal glowing affection but they lack the strong-willed wariness of a Rosalind or a Portia, and she and her lover must pay for her lack of faith in the power of mutual love. In short, she succumbs to social pressures which seek to repress and coerce her emotional life.

For Hamlet, the truly destructive circumstance is his mother's prompt marriage to the dead King's brother. This fact disquiets him and sets him apart from the marriage festivities even before he suspects Claudius of murder. With the characteristic desire, noted by Coleridge,[5] to abstract and generalize from particulars, he makes his mother's conduct an example of all womanhood: 'Frailty, thy name is woman!' (I.ii.146). His very desire 'not to think on't' drives him obsessively to dwell on her speed, posting to incestuous sheets with the physical 'dexterity' of a beast. The sane mind protests that there is more to marriage than sex, but Hamlet's range of perceptions has been narrowed by the event. Equally, his range of actions and feelings have been imprisoned by affairs of state which he could not have influenced.

If we may take the discussions between Ophelia and her father as being in chronological sequence, then during the two months between his father's death and his mother's marriage Hamlet's love-suit is still being seriously pursued. She shows no sign of recent neglect from him, and both she and her father repeat that he has wooed her 'of late' (I.iii.91, 99). The crucial change, then, comes when *she* neglects *him* at the counsel of her brother and father:

> *Polonius*: What, have you given him any hard words of late?
> *Ophelia*: No, my good lord; but, as you did command,
>   I did repel his letters, and denied
>   His access to me.
>   (II.i.107–9)

His apparent madness manifests itself in the familiar Burtonian symptoms of love melancholy,[6] clothes awry, his face pale, trembling and sighing so piteously and profoundly 'As it did seem to shatter all his bulk And end his being' (II.i.94–6). It is to Polonius' credit that he recognizes his misjudgment of Hamlet's motives and sees that the suit has been in earnest. But when saying that it is simply Ophelia's rejection that has made Hamlet mad, he is ignorant of the predisposed mental state of the young man caused by his mother's remarriage, the recent encounter with the ghost and the whole repressive machinery of Denmark's social and political life. Claudius suspects that there is more than meets the eye when he mutters, 'Love! His affections do not that way tend' (III.i.162). We cannot lightly brush aside the suggestion made by Nigel Alexander,[7] among others, that Hamlet's state is not caused by love but by his encounter with the ghost, but the ambiguity is built into the scene. Nor can we dismiss the possibility raised by Harold Goddard[8] that Ophelia's description of Hamlet's behaviour in her closet is a kind of hallucination. We can, however, suppose that she is beginning to perceive that her prior caution, no doubt a justified device for testing the sincerity of her lover, has gone horribly wrong, even though she is ignorant of the other matters troubling his mind.

Hamlet himself projects upon Ophelia the guilt and pollution he has found in Gertrude. Tossed helplessly between disillusionment, morbid fixation upon sex, and weary *ennui*, his tendency to draw all objects into the web of his imagination reveals itself in the way that he accuses Ophelia of his mother's apparent sin in the 'nunnery' scene. I do not want to retread ground covered by Harold Jenkins and J.M. Nosworthy among others[9] but since the strangeness of the nunnery scene lies in the seemingly erratic switches of tone adopted by Hamlet, an examination of them may help understanding. Ophelia enters as he is engrossed in a reflection on suicide ended by a resigned and rather soothing shrug about the meaninglessness of action. In such a mood it seems unlikely that his greeting of 'the fair Ophelia' holds any barb, for he is hardly aware of her presence. As she timidly tests the water with 'How does your honour?' she meets a civil enough reply. But when she raises the question of their terminated love affair by offering to redeliver the trinkets he had given her, it is not surprising that his hurt dignity should make him haughty:

> No, not I;
> I never gave you aught.
> (III.i.95–6)

Unwisely, she perseveres. In her gentle voice she reproaches Hamlet
for jilting her, and since she is the one who first denied him access
(II.i.109–10), his brittle composure snaps with surprise:

> Ha, ha! Are you honest?
> (III.i.103)

If she had been 'honest' in spurning him, then she cannot be 'honest'
now. She is, however, 'fair', and the solution to the conundrum is
that either honesty and beauty hold no discourse, or that the power
of beauty may transform honesty into a bawd. The second fits better
his mother's conduct which had initially suggested that 'paradox'
(III..114), and Ophelias's behaviour now 'gives it proof'. And since
her dishonesty is shared by his own mother, the terrible implication
is that he himself has inherited from 'our old stock' that very
dishonesty. Hence his certainty of another paradox: 'I did love you
once . . . I lov'd you not.' In a spirit of warning, he points out that if
she should breed by him she would be a breeder of sinners and the
only advice he can offer is that she should preserve her virginity by
going to a nunnery. If she marries, the old calumny will be prop-
agated. The only difference between a fool like her father and a wise
man is that the latter knows what he is doing:

> Or, if thou wilt needs marry, marry a fool; for wise men know
> well enough what monsters you make of them. To a nunnery go;
> and quickly too. Farewell.
> (III.i.138–40)

That women 'make of' men monsters bears both possible meanings,
to transform them into monsters (cuckolds) and produce monsters
(marred children) from them, and the implication is that the original
sin was woman's. The tangle of his thoughts about the supposed
wantonness, ignorance and duplicity of two women in particular
causes him to conflate them into a single identity, the Untrustwor-
thy Woman. Once again, however, the root of his confusion lies in
outside events which he cannot understand or control.

Hamlet's quick change in this scene from despair to a frenzy sustained in brutal bantering is shocking, but when closely examined its 'useless and wanton cruelty', as Dr Johnson calls it, is not inexplicable. We need no recourse to Dover Wilson's interpolated stage directions nor to an ironic reading of 'nunnery' as 'brothel'. On the other hand, the meaning cannot be understood by any one of the eavesdroppers for they, like Hamlet himself, are hampered by the limitations of their own points of view. They 'botch the words up fit to their own thoughts' (v.i.10), a habit adopted by all the political eavesdroppers throughout the play. Ophelia mingles pity for the noble mind of Hamlet, blasted with love into madness, with self-pity to find herself involved as the 'most deject and wretched' of ladies. She certainly cannot know what is in his mind.

Hamlet is too rawly sensitive to the pain caused him by the unwittingly irresponsible actions (as he sees them) of two women to endure the further pain of trying sympathetically to understand their feelings. To dull the pain he tries a brutal detachment from them, adopting a posture of swaggering toughness bred of burning resentment. It shows in the public glare of the 'mousetrap' scene in his short, sharp and bawdy retorts to Ophelia: 'Do you think I meant country matters?'; *Ophelia*: 'Tis brief, my lord. *Hamlet*: As woman's love'; 'So you mis-take your husbands?' (iii.ii.112–246 *passim*). Ophelia bears his taunts with patience yet with the occasional spirited response: 'You are naught, you are naught. I'll mark the play' (iii.ii.142–3). Hamlet's preoccupations are still sex and perversion of marriage by woman's infidelity, and the convergence of both in his words to Ophelia shows that he is still merging her identity with that of his mother. His mind is lacerated still further by the horror that his imagination can make of sex between his mother and Claudius, and so he confronts Gertrude:

> Nay, but to live
> In the rank sweat of an enseamed bed,
> Stew'd in corruption, honeying and making love
> Over the nasty sty!
> (iii.iv.91–4)

And again, even as he harangues the middle-aged woman, the younger is not far from his mind:

> Rebellious hell,
> If thou canst mutine in a matron's bones,
> To flaming youth let virtue be as wax
> And melt in her own fire; proclaim no shame
> When the compulsive ardour gives the charge,
> Since frost itself as actively doth burn,
> And reason panders will.
>
> (III.iv.82–8)

Female sexuality simultaneously frightens and fascinates him, and from these feelings he creates a stereotype that he affixes upon both his mother and Ophelia. The responsibility for the incomprehension is tangled and shared. Ophelia by her pliability, has set the process in motion, but Hamlet has subsequently distorted her behaviour so radically that the ground cannot be retrieved. One still cannot say, however, that the initial fault lies in either of those characters but in the total situation.

Ophelia's position after the death of Polonius is intolerable and cannot be faced directly without overwhelming mental pain. Her lover has forsaken and abused her, he has refused her trust, he has apparently gone mad and killed her own father. Worst of all, according to her father's ungenerous interpretation of prior events, her own conduct has been a precipitating cause of the whole sequence:

> But yet do I believe
> The origin and commencement of his grief
> Sprung from neglected love.
>
> (III.i.176–8)

For a girl wishing nobody harm, and one prone to selfless sympathy (III.i.150–61) the sense of implication is as bad as the events themselves. In order to defend her most sensitive feelings, and in order to make some sense of what has happened, Ophelia becomes distracted. The defence mechanism unconsciously discovered by her mind is to disappear into a world where such horrors are shared commonplaces — the world of the ballad.

> Thought and affliction, passion, hell itself,
> She turns to favour and to prettiness.
>
> (IV.v.184–5)

In the world of ballad, events like death and forsaken love are swung free from feelings of sharp pain and transformed into aesthetically pleasing patterns of rhythms and rhymes laced with archaic words, which supply the buffering reassurance of universal cycles. Even suffering becomes an aesthetic object, full of contemplated pathos, to be accepted or mocked but not to be experienced immediately on the pulses. More significantly, the ballad world frees individuals from guilt and responsibility, for it is peopled not with named characters but with 'he' and 'she'. Things simply happen because they have always happened and always will; human agents are accidental. We should be grateful that Ophelia's instincts for self-protection find such beautiful and appropriate refuge from rational awareness of her plight. She dies chanting snatches of old lauds, 'As one incapable of her own distress, Or like a creature native and indued Unto that element' (IV.vii.179–81). She has made herself safe from the bad dreams that plague Hamlet. We cannot condemn her retreat as in any way 'childish', for the ballad itself is surely 'adult' in its assertion of a fatalistic dignity in the face of pain, turning particular events into the shared memory of a community. Her words are disturbing to listeners, as if she speaks from a different realm (or even a different play), the inarticulate snatches growing to something of great constancy:

> Her speech is nothing,
> Yet the unshaped use of it doth move
> The hearers to collection: . . .
> (IV.v.7–9)

Laertes recognizes that 'This nothing's more than matter' (IV.v.171), but nobody can decipher its hieroglyphics.

By a kind of sympathetic magic, the conditions which face Ophelia find their way into her songs in oblique and confused fashion. Some snatches refer to her elderly father — 'He is dead and gone' — but the most consecutive song refers to forsaken love and reflects her own experience. There is an interesting switch of syntax from the personal to the impersonal. The song begins in the present tense — 'Tomorrow is Saint Valentine's day', and in the first person — 'And I a maid at your window, To be your Valentine' (IV.v.46–9). As if even this stylized expression is too close for comfort in tense and person, it changes to the past and to the third person:

Then up he rose, and donn'd his clothes,
And dupp'd the chamber-door;
Let in the maid, that out a maid
Never departed more.
(IV.v.50–3)

Here is the ballad mode and tone, implying that the event has
occurred not just once but many times from time immemorial. In
relation to Ophelia, the change has the added force that, although she
did stand outside Hamlet's door to be his Valentine, in fact she was
not allowed entrance. The part of her that wished to enter a sexual
relationship with him is personified in another 'maid'. The second
verse approaches the uncertain question. 'Whose fault?' In the
general scheme of things the man seems to be responsible:

Young men will do't, if they come to't,
By Cock, they are to blame.
(IV.v.58–9)

But the man cruelly transfers to her the blame for the broken
relationship by falling back on a quibble:

Quoth she, 'Before you tumbled me,
You promis'd me to wed'.

He answers:

'So would I 'a done, by yonder sun,
An thou hadst not come to my bed'.
(IV.v.60–4)

Although Ophelia undoubtedly dies a maid and is buried with her
virgin crants and maiden strewments (V.i.226–7), the song reflects
the equivocal nature of the break-up of the relationship, and surveys
the options she had. Did she forsake him, or he her? And if she had
been more forward and yielded her chastity to him instead of
succumbing to fear, would she not still have been discarded? On one
version of the facts, she has caused the rift by being too fearful to
pursue her love. But her love has been constant, and when she had
begun quietly to express it, she was rudely rebuffed and called a
whore, as if her declaration of love amounted to unchastity. Equally,
she must still be uncertain whether Hamlet was not throughout

cruelly dallying with her, as she had been warned. There is a problematical incompleteness in her experience of love, and the songs are an attempt to supply a dimension which will at least find an ending that has some meaning. The flowers she strews further emphasize the ambiguity of the unlived future, symbolizing on one side the past — memory and love-thoughts — on the other the potential pain of the future — flattery, cuckoldry, sorrow, repentance and dissembling. The flowers of faithfulness significantly ceased to be, after the traumatic event which destroyed her trust, when her lover killed her father:

> I would give you some violets, but they wither'd all, when my father died . . .
> (IV.v.181)

One hopes that Laertes speaks prophetically in his benediction over her grave:

> Lay her i' th' earth;
> And from her fair and unpolluted flesh
> May violets spring!
> (v.i.232–4)

The Queen's elegiac dirge-description of the death of Ophelia shows her own capacity for intuitively reaching into the feelings of another character and touching them with beauty. The rhythms of her poetry, like the folds of the maiden's clothing, hold and hang her suspended upon the water's surface:

> Her clothes spread wide
> And mermaid-like, awhile they bore her up;
> (IV.vii.176–7)

while Ophelia's ballad allows her to rise above 'her own distress' with the same buoyancy. Against the upward pressure the tug of the water is a violation of her floating purity:

> but long it could not be
> Till that her garments, heavy with their drink,
> Pull'd the poor wretch from her melodious lay
> To muddy death.
> (IV.vii.181–4)

The placing of 'Pull'd' and the loading of 'heavy with their drink' turn poignant regret into dismay, just as does the juxtapositioning of 'clamb'ring to hang' and 'Fell in the weeping brook'. Ophelia dies beneath the willow, the Elizabethan emblem for forsaken love,[10] a fit motif for her life as well as her death.

The lyrical adagio of Ophelia's death is followed abruptly by the grave-diggers' legal quibbles about whether she committed suicide, whether she came to the water or the water came to her, in terms of the celebrated law case.[11] It is significant that Hamlet's entrance is greeted by a snatch of song from the grave-digger, and the mode and subject-matter recall Ophelia's songs. The first verse celebrates the carefree sweetness of love in youth, the second contrasts age, whose stealing steps have clawed him in its clutch as if he had never been young. Hamlet himself has acquired a new voice, more controlled and reflective, less self-tortured. At thirty[12] he can hardly be the man who was emphatically 'young' when courting Ophelia (I.iii.7, 41, 124), young enough to be suspected of irresponsibly sowing his wild oats in carefree youth. He now has the self-possession to regret his outburst against Laertes in the grave (v.ii.73–9), and to accept his destiny as part of the way of the world:

> . . . the readiness is all. Since no man owes of aught he leaves
> what is't to leave betimes? Let be.
>   (v.ii.215–6)

It may be the last lesson that his lover, by her death, has taught him, and if so, then her frustrated life is given another value. In the grave-digger's song the aged lover may well renounce his love, but such a jaunty recollection of the past is as much an insult to Ophelia's faith in love as are the 'maimed' rites accorded her body by a grudging priest and the unseemly scuffle in her grave between Hamlet and Laertes. At last there is occasion for Hamlet to recognize unequivocally his own feelings with the rushing rhythms of spontaneous emotion:

> I lov'd Ophelia; forty thousand brothers
> Could not, with all their quantity of love,
> Make up my sum.
>   (v.i.263–5)

Despite the value given to Ophelia's tragedy by the purposefulness that it unleashes in Hamlet, her death remains a sacrifice to the general meaninglessness and loneliness pervading the play. In the world of comedy, lovers' tribulations take meaning from a consummation within their lifetime instead of after their death. When Viola in *Twelfth Night* speaks of herself as the neglected lover who 'never told her love, But let concealment, like a worm i' th' bud Feed on her damask cheek' (*Twelfth Night*, II.iv.109–11) we know that her instincts will be answered, the past redeemed and misunderstanding cleared up. In the world of comedy the path from innocence to experience is gently guided by circumstances. But in *Hamlet* the past is responsible for the future to the bitter end. Ophelia is the loser. Unlike Blake's Thel she has had no kind and matronly guide into the land of sexual experience and her desire to see 'the secrets of the land unknown' (*The Book of Thel*, plate 6) is a lonely and fearful quest which leaves her at the end still on the threshold. Ophelia's own words, wry rather than bitter, show some comprehension of what has happened: 'Lord, we know what we are, but know not what we may be' (IV.v.41).

Like Hamlet himself, Ophelia is destroyed, slowly and remorselessly, by the nature of the society in which she finds herself. Unlike the man, she is given no indication of the murder of old Hamlet which set the tragic events in motion, and she is faced with a puzzling and frightening world of emotional and political coercion, a world where everybody spies on neighbours and where the undercurrent of personal violence in relationships is all the more palpable for being repressed and hidden behind a façade of courtly politeness. Her personality unformed and her nature co-operative, she has no single point of view from which to assess situations, and she has no capacity for independent action because of her place in society. The result for her, and again for Hamlet in a different way, is growing alienation and isolation. Her final snatches of song come as the desperate cries of a lonely soul, adrift from any anchor of certainty, seeking communication and help in making sense of such an opaquely contradictory society. Shakespeare has dignified her loneliness with scenes so moving that they cannot be ignored, explained away, or forgotten in the ways that the implicated characters carry out to their own satisfaction. For many in an audience, there is nothing to match in emotional intensity the pathos evoked by Ophelia's tragedy, and even the hero himself cannot stir such unequivocal feelings of pity and fear. It needs no special pleading, then, to see her history as being centrally connected with the significance of the play as a whole. She has awakened her lover to outraged action against the whole system that corrupts Denmark, and if she can awaken also in us a sense of the futility and cruelty of her death, a more precise analysis of the forces that destroy her, and a recognition of the peaceful alternative of trusting love which she has intuitively practised, then supreme value can be retrieved from the fact of her death. In Shakespeare's Elsinore the 'inset'[13] tragedy of Ophelia is not an isolated phenomenon to be analysed purely in terms of the character's psychological make-up. It is an exemplary emblem of the victimization and official secrecy of a whole political world headed by a corrupt monarch. An awareness of her suffering certainly leads us into emotions such as sympathy but it also leads us outwards into a clear-eyed moral scrutiny of the society in which she lives and dies.

VII Desdemona

To many the death of Desdemona poses no particular difficulty of interpretation. It is simply a *datum* of the play, forced upon Shakespeare by his sources.[1] Since the tradition of modern criticism has concentrated upon the mental suffering of the 'great man' in tragedy, there is never room for exploring the moral world of the play from the victim's point of view (except insofar as Othello is seen as a victim). Such a view is generally discounted as insignificant. However, if we do choose to concentrate upon the death of Desdemona, we find ourselves confronting fundamental issues of justice in a society which has a vested interest in ignoring or covering up injustice. Whether our consciences are awakened for only a moment, or whether we are lucky in learning a more lasting lesson, our feelings must be activated to the outrage so powerfully expressed by Emilia:

> Nay, lay thee down and roar;
> For thou hast kill'd the sweetest innocent
> That e'er did lift up eye.
> (v.ii.201–3)

It is important to realize that the problems raised by the death of Desdemona need not be seen as a particularly modern or anachronistic preoccupation. One of the extremely rare and valuable records of contemporary responses to Shakespeare's plays by an Elizabethan audience concerns *Othello*, without even mentioning the great man himself. Henry Jackson wrote in September, 1610:

> *At vero Desdemona illa apud nos a marito occisa, quamquam optime semper causam egit, interfecta tamen magis movebat; cum in lecto decumbens spectantium misericordiam ipso vultu imploraret.*[2]

The pity of the spectators was invoked by the sight of Desdemona lying on the bed, and this was apparently the most moving part of the play. Eighteenth-century critics, for all their deficiencies, at least recognized acutely the existence of problems in poetic justice. The attempts to rewrite the endings to many of Shakespeare's plays may

seem ludicrous now, but they were carried out with principled
intentions. They were based on the classical assumption that literature should show what *ought* to happen in a fully moral world, rather
than the fortuitous arbitrariness of what actually *does* happen in life.
The world of nature is 'brazen, the poets only deliver a golden', as
Sidney puts it, and he insists that writers should exercise a moral
control over the created work. For this reason eighteenth-century
critics worried much more than we do about the deaths of Cordelia
and Desdemona. Perhaps they were fortunate in not having a
treacherously conditioned myth of 'survival of the fittest', which is
our own unlucky legacy from the commercially predatory
nineteenth century and allows us to accept such injustices. On the
death of Desdemona, Dr Johnson, with his acute moral faculty,
wrote simply 'It is not to be endured'. It is interesting that he finds
fault with Shakespeare rather than with Venetian society, for creating the atrocity. On the lines 'This sorrow's heavenly; It strikes
where it doth love' (v.ii.21–2) spoken by Othello after the deed,
Johnson writes, 'I wish these two lines could be honestly ejected. It is
the fate of Shakespeare to counteract his own pathos'. Presumably he
is criticizing Shakespeare for giving the audience an easy way out of
its feeling of outrage, by putting into Othello's mouth a self-
justificatory and rationalizing doctrine of 'heavenly suffering'. The
line would particularly gall the Christian Johnson, for its near
blasphemy.[3] It is constantly observed throughout this book, however, that the great man and his society will always collude in such an
exercise of rationalization, and that such a strategy is calculated by
the speakers to counteract in their own minds the guilt created by an
innocent's death. Unlike Johnson, Shakespeare must have trusted
his audiences to be morally awake, and to hold on to the feeling of
outrage which is voiced so decisively by Emilia. Thomas Rymer's
indignation carries a real force, when he deals with Desdemona: 'If
this be our end, what boots it to be virtuous?' but the 'moral' he
finds, that young women should not disobey their fathers, is probably the most insensitive example on record of the critic's congenital
desire to blame the victim and condone the forces of prescriptive
authority.

Nineteenth-century critics were distressed too, but on the rather
different ground that they saw the ending of this play as an affront to
our feelings. It is clear that they are talking not primarily about

Desdemona but about the mental suffering experienced by Othello. They feel that a man who loved so well does not deserve such torment. The editor of the Variorum Shakespeare, first published in 1886, writes in a footnote, 'I do not shrink from saying that I wish this Tragedy had never been written. The pleasure, however keen or elevated, which the inexhaustible poetry of the preceding Acts can bestow, cannot possibly, to my temperament, countervail, it does but increase, the unutterable agony of this closing Scene.'[4] Bradley simply says that, if played by a great actor and a great actress, the last scene would be 'pronounced intolerable'.[5] The best that our own century can do, apparently, is to emphasize another nineteenth-century rationalization as insulting and authoritarian as Rymer's that Desdemona 'deserves' to die because she tells a wicked lie. Despite the attractiveness of such logic and amorality to a sophisticated audience, such an approach depends on a dangerous avoidance of any emotional engagement with the play. It cauterizes the moral imagination altogether. By emphasizing the laws of strict logic, and ignoring the involvement of feelings, we are fully committing ourselves to the party of Iago. Before making judgments, we should seek to understand each of the characters as sympathetically as possible, and examine the sequence of events as presented in the play, where a complex moral situation is enacted between three equally important people.

In Act I, Shakespeare unobtrusively builds up a network of themes and associations which are to be relentlessly developed in the rest of the action. Indeed, the oppressive beauty of the play comes partly from the fact that no detail is ever left alone. The inexorable consequences of each come with Hardyesque fatality. For our purposes, a strand which deserves attention is the clear definition of two opposing attitudes towards justice, and to the kind of moral responsibility which a person exercises over the future. Both Iago and Othello are aware of a shadowy future that will unfold itself in time, composed of both 'accidents' (a word used five times by four characters), voluntary actions and logical causation. The future is described as 'many events in the womb of time which will be delivered' (I.iii.367), but the manner of delivery may be seen in different lights. Both Othello and Iago believe in 'fate', but in quite different senses. On the one hand, life may be seen as a series of unexpected accidents and strange chances, arbitrary and random events that have no special logic, except the logic of coincidence and miracle. On the other hand, one can perceive an 'answerable seques-tration' (I.iii.347), as Iago puts it, a chain of causation which makes every occurrence a rigorous consequence of its predecessors. Appar-ent accidents may then be interpreted as 'foregone conclusions' (III.iii.432), a phrase used perhaps for the first time in our language in *Othello*, when the Moor has been infected by Iago's point of view. It might be surmised that the man of military endeavour living his life on the high seas will see 'fate' in the light of chance and accident, whilst the city-bred person, closely enmeshed in a society which he knows inside out, will be tempted to see fate more cautiously, as a matter of incremental and largely predictable change, which may be partly controlled by exercise of the 'purse'.

The event which precipitates the action of the play, the marriage, can be seen from both points of view, and it is. Knowledge of it bursts upon Venetian society like a thunderstorm, and it is seen as an unexpected and shocking natural calamity. Brabantio sees it as an 'accident', and the fact that he has foreseen it in a dream only emphasizes the element of the supernatural. The only explanation for the society is that the event has been caused by witchcraft and magic. But when we hear the self-assured, stately account of the wooing by Othello, and the dignified verification spoken by Desde-mona, we see that it has occurred over a long period and is predict-able if only in the sense that 'one thing leads to another'. As the Duke says, 'I think this tale would win my daughter too' (I.iii.171), and Brabantio himself has aided and abetted the development of a 'foregone conclusion' by treating with such paternal respect and familial hospitality a character like Othello. We hear other, more grubby explanations for the romance from others, and particularly Iago, who can understand only the logic of lust between two romantically deluded beasts. To him, there is no wonderful unex-pectedness, but only the predictable notion that an old black ram will seek to tup a white ewe, and that a foolish, pretty young woman will lust after an attractive officer, whether it be Othello or Cassio.

Othello is the one who most readily sees his life in terms of accidents, luck and unlucky changes. He is accustomed to take things as they come, without questioning and without searching for causes, until he falls prey to Iago's confident attitudes. At the beginning, Othello relies upon an ultimate and external moral judgment upon his actions. Seeing his life as a 'pilgrimage' in which he will face 'disastrous chances . . . moving accidents' and 'hairbreadth 'scapes i' th' imminent deadly breach', in which he will act spontaneously as he thinks fit without circumspection or cautious calculation, he is confident that if his actions are virtuous then he will find 'redemption' and if not then he must face an eternal punishment:

> My parts, my title, and my perfect soul
> Shall manifest me rightly.
> (I.ii.31–2)

The tragedy for him is that his philosophy, forged in a life of decisive action in war, must now be tested in the thorny territory of a sophisticated and expedient society, in which he seeks to conduct a personal relationship. He is deceived into forfeiting his philosophy, which amounts to losing himself, at least in the eyes of an observer, Lodovico:

> Is this the noble Moor whom our full Senate
> Call all in all sufficient? Is this the nature
> Whom passion could not shake, whose solid virtue
> The shot of accident nor dart of chance
> Could neither graze nor pierce?
> *Iago*: He is much chang'd.
> (IV.i.261–6)

The change, over which Iago gloats so appreciatively, is largely caused by his own success in unsettling the firm confidence of Othello's beliefs. Iago is the thoroughly Newtonian man, believing that for every effect there is a cause, and once in possession of information, then we can control the future even of others. His plot to make Othello jealous is based on this attitude, as he carefully plans each step, calculating the consequences every moment, resting on the assumption that we live in a deterministic universe where everything is predictable to the man who is in possession of the facts. His morality, his sense of justice, springs from a consistently rationalistic source. He believes that we can and must exercise 'will' to shape our destinies, and the question of ultimate judgment of good and bad is subsidiary to the quest for social respectability and power in the short term:

> Virtue? A fig! 'Tis in ourselves that we are thus or thus. Our
> bodies are our gardens to the which our wills are gardeners; so
> that if we will plant nettles or sow lettuce, set hyssop and weed up
> thyme, supply it with one gender of herbs or distract it with
> many, either to have it sterile with idleness or manur'd with
> industry — why, the power and corrigible authority lies in our
> wills.   (I.iii.320–5)

We need not here seek for the psychological and social factors that
make Iago the person he is, but to sharpen the contrast we can say
that Iago is represented as the 'new man' (a myth that may exist in
every generation to condone the lesser virtues of social respectability, power, and unfeeling oppression over others). He is worldly (in
his own narrow world), and sophisticated, and his ideas have been
formed in an urban realm where competition, self-reliance and
manipulation may lead to promotion, 'reputation' in the eyes of
one's own society, and all the ensuing commercial benefits. To an
Iago, Othello's beliefs are simply a recipe for unprofessional attitudes and an obscure life, when practised by one with no particular
physical endowments nor social advantages. Othello, however,
comes from a past that contained Everyman and the medieval
moralities, where the true moral sanctions are spiritual rather than
expedient. The divergence of critical opinion over Othello in modern times perhaps stems from the fact that he strikes us as somewhat
old-fashioned, and we are always ambiguously poised between
admiration and contempt for a simpler, safer, grander past.[6] It is
interesting also, in terms of the design of the play, to see that the
initial strengths and weaknesses of each character exactly balance
each other. Where Othello is strong (at the beginning and end) in his
profoundly felt sense of justice and true morality which is appallingly eroded by Iago, the latter is non-existent as a truly moral force. On
the other hand, where Iago is the expert 'plotter' over events, using
all the skills of a dramatist in his close observation of verisimilitude,
Othello is hopelessly weak, for he sees himself guided by larger
forces out of his control (as, one should add, he is).

The contrasting attitudes to justice held by Othello and Iago are
relevant here insofar as they determine the ways in which the two
characters view Desdemona. To Othello, the fact that she fell in love
with him was a marvellous miracle for which he could take no

personal credit, but which in some way was a divine reward for his virtue. She has sanctified his past adventures, giving them a dignity which comes from her concern and wonder. There is no explicit acknowledgment of physical attraction on either side. She trustingly says: 'I saw Othello's visage in his mind' (I.iii.252), while he says.

> She lov'd me for the dangers I had pass'd;
> And I lov'd her that she did pity them.
> (I.iii.167–8)

Desdemona's feelings, judging from her words, come from decisive attraction to him, allured as she is by the romantic glamour of the events in Othello's life, which she hears through his poetic language. He in his turn seems to be attracted by the domestic, sheltered, conciliatory life of Desdemona, so alien to him and revealed to him in her 'pity'. The way he notices her little household routines may betray some fascination:

> But still the house affairs would draw her thence;
> Which ever as she could with haste dispatch,
> She'd come again . . .
> (I.iii.147–9)

He may be capable of drawing her into his own linguistic circuit by addressing her as 'My fair warrior' and she may be capable of domesticating him as 'My dear Othello', but such endearing pet-phrases may at this stage of the play be affectionate attempts to accommodate the otherness of the beloved into a personal language, rather than an ominous sign of potential 'miscomprehension', as John Bayley suggests.[7] Their love is mutual, conscious and out-spoken.

Iago finds the explanation given by Othello and Desdemona for their love quite unconvincing. In his desire to find 'realistic' reasons for everything, he simply cannot accept that the attraction is anything but physical and sexual: 'It is merely a lust of the blood and a permission of the will' (I.iii.333). He sees the consequences as logically predictable.

> She must change for youth; when she is sated with his body, she will find the error of her choice.
> (I.iii.350)

Iago genuinely sees Desdemona not as a sympathetic woman whose
world has revolved around the routine occupation of the home, but
as a volatile creature of flesh and blood with powerful sexual desires
which lead her to initiate sexual contact. In his eyes she is 'full of
game', with an eye which 'sounds a parley to provocation' (II.iii.19–
21). He makes the same mistake about her as Claudio makes of Hero
in *Much Ado About Nothing*, as Hamlet makes of Ophelia and
Gertrude and as, (I would argue), the Greeks make of Cressida when
they believe that 'Nay, her foot speaks' simply because she is an
attractive woman.[8] In each case, the fault lies in the man for
imposing a stereotype upon the woman. There is absolutely no
evidence in her words or conduct to provide a shred of evidence for
Iago's vision, nor Othello's when he grows jealous, but Iago's
conviction of Desdemona's lustiness breathes into almost every
word he speaks about her. Most obviously, he makes suggestive
comments to Othello about her capriciousness, and he also fantasizes
about bedding her with Cassio and Roderigo. His provocative,
bawdy songs to her, while they await the arrival of Othello from
Cyprus, are calculated to draw out her own presumed salaciousness,
and although she politely acknowledges the badinage, she also
confides in an aside her weariness with the conversation:

> I am not merry; but I do beguile
> The thing I am by seeming otherwise.
> (II.i.122–3)

Of course, some insensitive critics have used the comment as
evidence that she is consistently devious and dissimulating, but such
an opinion ignores the obvious function of her comment, to distance
her from Iago's attitudes while maintaining her loyal desire to
co-operate in a conversation whose direction she cannot control. She
is trapped in a world where the sinister advice of Iago which he
significantly repeats during the play, 'be a man!' (I.iii.333 and
IV.i.65) draws our attention to the dominant creed, a world where
the woman must satisfy the man in all activities or be denounced like
Emilia as a shrew. (Again, it would be a culturally interesting fact if
this phrase were coined in its modern sense in our language by this
devil of a man.)

In the middle of the play, Iago, exploiting the coloured alien's fear
that he is ignorant of the subtle manners, customs and codes of

Venetian society, challenges Othello's reliance upon the poetic justice of ultimate reward for virtue.[9] He does so by harping on the string that is fatal to any of our ideals, suggesting they are 'not realistic', not 'the way of the world', not 'being a man'. From what we have seen of their characters, we can understand not only why Iago is always suggesting that there must be rational 'causes' for every tiny event (even the loss of a handkerchief), but also why Othello's very idealism makes him vulnerable to such a strategy. A statement like 'This honest creature doubtless Sees and knows more — much more than he unfolds' (III.iii.246–7), shows how much Othello has been persuaded to trust Iago's knowledge of areas in which Othello confesses ignorance, the knowledge of cause and effects in society. Cleverly, Iago challenges Othello's main assumption, by suggesting that the marriage was not such a miraculously unpredictable event, but simply the result of a spirited young woman's rebellion against parental control: 'She did deceive her father, marrying you' (III.iii.210). Here is direct evidence that if we should begin to criticize Desdemona's deceptions as a fatal vice rather than judging from her conduct, we are falling straight into Iago's camp and thereby relinquishing ideals and moral instincts. Harping on the tiny word 'cause', Iago drives Othello into an agony of wishing to see the very cause itself, the 'ocular proof' of adultery. The strawberry-coloured handkerchief, to be associated by imagery with a deranged vision of Desdemona's bed 'lust-stained with lust's blood spotted' (v.i.36), takes on a strangely double function, like the little flower love-in-idleness in *A Midsummer Night's Dream*. At one and the same time it is a magical talisman ensuring fidelity and virtue, given to Othello by his mother for his future wife, and now a fatal link in a chain of causation created by Iago in order to incriminate Desdemona. In Iago's hands the handkerchief is given a new personality, mocking Othello's idealism and principles, as if it has betrayed him by actively changing sides in a debate on morality. Similarly, love-in-idleness acquires a whimsically mischievous personality when handled by Puck, as he applies it to the eyes of the wrong lovers. The irony, of course, is that the loss of the handkerchief, like Puck's misapplication, is an 'accident' in Othello's old sense of the word which should be cleared up by the comic divinities of passing time, fortuitous revelation, and moral deserts.

Othello's moral precept that virtue must be allowed to triumph of its own accord is shattered by Iago's deterministic view that the individual can do something about the future by exercising his will. In a grotesque conflation of his old belief in moral retribution and his newly acquired sense that destiny is no more than a chain of causes and effects, Othello now takes upon himself an active role. He begins to apply his will as a living avenger, a scourge of vice, on behalf of higher arbiters of morality. Convinced that in a deterministic society he should not leave it up to supernatural powers, he accepts the role of administrator of justice in this world.

> Arise, black vengeance, from the hollow hell.
> (III.iii.451)

> Yet she must die, else she'll betray more men.
> (v.ii.6)

> O balmy breath, that must almost persuade
> Justice to break her sword!
> (v.ii.16)

There is a revealing ambiguity in his hypnotic, somnambulistic words as he approaches Desdemona, taper in hand, as a candle to light her to bed, to kill her:

> It is the cause, it is the cause, my soul —
> Let me not name it to you, you chaste stars —
> It is the cause.
> (v.ii.1–3)

'Cause' is a word learned from Iago, and Othello is using it in two senses: He must kill her *because* of a rationally ordered set of circumstances which, if not halted would lead to misery for more men. And he must kill her *as a cause*, a religious or charitable mission, on behalf of ultimate powers of morality. In seeking to understand the respective attitudes of Othello and Iago, we need neither condemn nor condone the *motives* of the former, though we must condemn his action. But men are responsible for a murder, and no matter what justification or explanations may be found, the act itself, irrespective of motives, is evil. To Othello's credit, he acknowledges this by the end, in a return to his more stable self, reiterating his old creed that we must stand judged by our actions.[10] The real tragedy is not that of the great man who must suffer in the mind for his misdeeds and commit suicide. It is the fate of the misunderstood, murdered woman, who has been given no true place in the world of such 'great' men.

We should look now at Desdemona herself, not as she is seen by others, but as she expresses herself. Her very name, from the Greek for 'unfortunate', links her with potential injustice, and her line 'It is my wretched fortune' (IV.ii.129) has a despairing ring to it. Unlike the male characters, she is not given to abstract philosophizing. As Mrs Jameson remarked in 1832, it is a peculiarity of Desdemona that she never gives voice to 'general observations', although Mrs Jameson is ungenerous in putting this down to an absence of 'intellectual power' in the character.[11] She is also marked by a complete innocence in word and deed. Cassio, baited by Iago, may suspect in her 'An inviting eye', but even such a man-about-town as he respectfully adds 'and yet methinks right modest' (II.iii.22). The modesty is borne out by her speech. She endures Iago's bawdy, insinuating talk with embarrassed disapproval, forced to hide her real feelings of sadness at Othello's absence in a show of sociability. She valiantly keeps up a brave face of gentle politeness even when she prepares the feast for her husband's guests after she has been humiliated and struck by him in public. Her patient acceptance of a need to cover up her feelings in public is certainly a central trait, but on each occasion that she 'beguiles' the thing she is, it is done in order to preserve social harmony or to protect the position or sensitivities of somebody else. She is forced by all those around her, and compelled by her own desire for peace, to be diplomatic. She is a true 'moth of peace'. Her range of tones reveals more of her character. There is the sturdy commitment to her love in the face of parental and potentially state disapproval, and there is her outspoken defence of Emilia when Iago insults her: 'O, fie upon thee, slanderer!' (II.i.113), as well as the innocent bemusement of her question to a more experienced female confidante:

> Dost thou in conscience think — tell me, Emilia —
> That there be women do abuse their husbands
> In such a gross kind?
> (IV.iii.59–61)

Her sigh, 'O, these men, these men' (IV.iii.58) in which she unwittingly echoes Iago's 'But men are men' (II.iii.233), is the closest she gets to a general observation on a situation into which she has been uncomprehendingly coerced, and it is completely consistent with her character in its patient sorrow and its refusal to complain or blame. Her most recurrent tone is one of domestic complaisance in phrases like 'What e'er you be, I am obedient' (III.iii.90), and her imagery is full of common decencies such as meal-times, nourishing dishes, or putting on warm gloves when it is cold. Her one moment of admiration for a man other than her husband is couched in terms of respect and propriety, and it is Emilia who reads into it a sexual innuendo that reflects her own attitudes rather than those of her mistress:

> *Desdemona*: This Lodovico is a proper man.
> *Emilia*: A very handsome man.
> *Desdemona*: He speaks well.
>   (IV.iii.34–6)

When she asks Iago what would be the reward given to a 'deserving woman . . . in the authority of her merits' (a language she may have heard from the 'early' Othello himself), she meets a rude and dismissive answer: 'To suckle fools and chronicle small beer' (II.i.159). It is not necessary or true to say that Desdemona is presented as a stereotype of femininity, for there is enough in the detail of the play to find the reasons why she is as she is. In a male world of 'reputation', 'honour', competitiveness, statecraft and war — the world of the 'great man' — her *human* capacities for trust, sympathy and self-effacement are disregarded and demeaned, while false images of lust and promiscuousness are foisted upon her. It is not only her character but the world around her that occasionally force her to prevaricate and try to avoid conflict where there seems no need for any. Her famous 'lie' about the handkerchief, 'It is not lost; but what an if it were?' (III.iv.83) which gets her into so much trouble with critics who pride themselves on being stern moralists, can be turned rapidly against a society and a maliciously created set of circumstances that force a person into such impossible predicaments. Of course she lacks the outspoken forthrightness and independence of a Cordelia, but again we can say that her particular society does not even notice when she does stand up for herself. After Othello strikes her she maintains 'I have not deserv'd this' (again, a comment which Othello himself, if uncontaminated by

Iago and Venice would respect), but she is violently attacked.

As the play goes on, Desdemona is increasingly trapped in the position of dovelike victim, completely ignorant of the lies which have been spread around her, and temperamentally committed to protecting the feelings of others before her own. Her simple words 'Unpin me here' catch the passivity and vulnerability which she has displayed throughout. The 'willow song', in the scene probably meant by the contemporary Henry Jackson, beautifully catches and defines in a moment of wistful stasis the pathos of her situation. In the indirectness of its simple parable, and its hushed, melodic control, the song provides a unique moment of fragile peace in a play marked from its opening moments by quarrels, storms, war, banished music (III.i.9–20), disturbed sleep. (On at least three occasions in the play sleep is violently broken into, and this seems highly significant.) The song gives a poignant premonition of Desdemona's last words in the play, as once again she tries to protect others:

> Sing all a green willow must be my garland.
> Let nobody blame him; his scorn I approve —
> Nay, that's not next . . .
> (IV.iii.49–51)

However loath she is to express herself in generalizations, Desdemona reveals consistently, every time she speaks and acts, a very firm vision of the world, based on mutual co-operation. It is not her fault that the world around her is adept at the lies, distortions, calculated misunderstandings and wilful ignorance that marks its ruthlessly competitive acceptance of the values of power politics. Like Ophelia, she is forced to speak her feelings obliquely, in the allegory of ballad; and like Lucrece she accepts a blame, a shame, which has been wrongly pinned upon her by her surrounding circumstances and by male dominance. .

As in *King Lear*, Shakespeare keeps our hopes for a happy ending fluttering almost to the end. First, Iago, after the terrifying and chilling black mass in which he swears allegiance to Othello in deeds of death, says of Cassio:

> My friend is dead;
> 'Tis done at your request. But let her live.
> (III.iii.477–9)

It may be a ploy to make Othello direct his mind to killing Desdemona, but on the other hand it reminds us of Iago's own designs on the woman, and perhaps it gives us a cause to hope that his vindictiveness will be confined to Cassio and to the torment he has already created in Othello. (It is Iago, however, who later suggests the strangling of Desdemona.) Secondly, the edifice of evidence and potential disaster built upon the loss of a handkerchief is so much a *comic* misunderstanding, and so slenderly based, that audiences find it difficult to believe fully that a death will hang on it. Even up to the moment when she is smothered, Desdemona is crying out that Othello should investigate the evidence more closely, confident of her innocence and baffled by ignorance. It is recorded that on one or two occasions in its stage history, members of the audience witnessing *Othello* ran on to the stage to remonstrate, because the reversal to a happy ending would be so easy, appropriate and just. Thirdly, Desdemona pleads desperately for time — for a night, a half hour, time for one prayer — and although a memory of *Doctor Faustus* may give us cause to fear that the dramatist will not be merciful, yet Desdemona has not sinned as Faustus has, and we feel that the revelation of truth may come at any moment. All that is needed is time for Emilia, the voice of our moral feelings, to enter, and she is at this moment hammering on the door. Finally, as if to tease us still further, after Desdemona has been smothered and Emilia has entered, Shakespeare brings Desdemona back to life, not once but twice. First she whispers, 'O falsely, falsely murdered!' The words, in the past tense, come from a voice beyond the grave, but we feel a rush of hope, and Emilia's response heightens it:

> Help! Help! ho! help! O lady, speak again!
> Sweet Desdemona! O sweet mistress, speak!
>   (v.ii.123–4)

And she does indeed speak again. These revivals leave yet a tiny possibility of another. But as in *Lear*, each possibility is dashed as soon as it is raised. To Iago's request that she live, Othello vows death on the 'fair devil'; to Desdemona's protests about the handkerchief, Othello retorts that she is perjuring herself; to her plea for more time he says simply, 'Too late'; and after her final words (to which we shall return), the reader of a modern edition (but not the First Folio) is aware, as an audience is not, of the fatal little stage direction, '*She dies*'. The effect of these shreds of hope differs from the effect in *Lear*. Gloucester and Cordelia both die off-stage, as if the play has forgotten about them in the belief that their problems have been solved, and the news comes as a devastating shock, with no time for suspense. Here, in the awful constriction of the darkened room and the bed, the effect is an accentuation of the play-world, embodied in Othello's action, relentlessly strangling all vestiges of life out of the heroine. What is the dramatic purpose of such victimization? Surely it cannot *simply* be to make more touching the terrible remorse and self-recrimination of Othello when he 'wakes up', and make us feel sorry for his suffering within. What he is awakened to is something that we have already long ago perceived, frightening faults and blindnesses in the society in which Othello himself has been inveigled to participate. The pain may be all the greater, and our anger may be somewhat softened towards Othello himself by his instant and full repentance, but our anger must be stirred, as is Emilia's, all the more towards Iago and the society of which he is a conditioned product. We need not pass judgment on Othello, nor need we squabble about whether he has been throughout a self-aggrandizing fool or a magnanimous figure whose feelings are misdirected. He has been changed by the malevolent pressures put upon him, and our moral instincts are tested out in their capacity to recognize the change, and understand the reasons which are not entirely to do with his own character. His repentance at the end should give us some relief (even if it will not bring Desdemona back to life), and heighten our outrage at the forces outside him which drove him to the deed.

To return from the questions of sympathy to more general problems of poetic justice, we can conclude that each person dies 'in character' reasserting fundamental attitudes. Desdemona's first 'last words' are, 'A guiltless death I die', and in answer to Emilia's question, 'O who hath done this deed?' she replies, 'Nobody: I myself. Farewell. Commend me to my kind lord. O, Farewell'. (v.ii.125–8). In her first sentence she is establishing not only her own innocence but also exonerating all others from blame. The second statement is curious. Othello (and unsympathetic critics) pick it up as further evidence of her congenital tendency to perjure herself: 'She's like a liar gone to burning hell: 'Twas I that kill'd her' (v.ii.132–3). We cannot avoid detecting a note of triumph at the proof of her untrustworthiness, and also petulant self-righteousness in the fear that the credit for his triumph is being taken away from him. By saying 'Nobody', perhaps Desdemona is recognizing that Othello acted, in legal parlance, with diminished responsibility owing to provocation of which she is not aware. When she adds 'I myself', however, she introduces a more complex notion. She may have realized that her own actions have somehow contributed to her death, although she can hardly have much evidence for this. She may even, to countenance momentarily one of the most disgraceful of all modern myths, be a person who unconsciously but willingly invites violence, as one who, unable to retain the affection of her lover, prefers to suffer pain at his hands. The third explanation is the most attractive, since it allows us to recognize Desdemona's consistency of thought and action, and does not imply that she is fully aware of the train of events leading up to the death. She is taking upon herself the whole blame, although she knows she is not personally guilty, as a self-sacrificial gesture to exonerate and forgive her husband. Without pretentiousness, with her usual self-effacement and desire to protect the consciences and feelings of others, Desdemona has taken upon herself the mantle of martyr. As Lucrece's suicide was a paradox of innocence acquiring shame, so is Desdemona's final statement, and perhaps the comparison shows that the martyr's position is always paradoxical. She is dying *for* others. Guiltless herself, she takes upon herself the guilt. Innocent, she accepts personal blame, in the hope that her gesture may liberate any remaining good impulses in others. It is to such a paradoxical pass that the concept of poetic justice has been driven when relentlessly pursued by a rival code based on causality, expedience and public reputation. Perhaps the greatest truths, when attacked by the forces of rationalism and rationalization, can be expressed *only* in paradox, a fact of which most religions and mysticism are well aware.

Desdemona's faith in the consequences of her statement is not ill-founded. The effect of her death is in turn to bring Othello back to the principles of justice which he had espoused long before. We suddenly realize that *Othello* is not entirely different from other love tragedies in that both lovers are, in varying degrees, victims of social forces. Othello has been deluded and perverted in as great a measure as Desdemona has been wronged, and although guilty as the agent of destruction by his own hands, he recovers some integrity of spirit by confessing his wrongdoing⌋ After the knot of misunderstandings has been unravelled by the exposure of Iago's evil, Othello resorts again to his philosophy that it is the way a man copes with accidents and 'unlucky deeds' that defines his moral deserts. He acknowledges the terrible mistake he has made when he was persuaded by a mortal that he can take upon himself the role of divine avenger: 'O vain boast! Who can control his fate' (v.ii.267–8). He regains sufficient objectivity to give a masterly summary of his own deserts. In war, he has done the state some service, and deserves a measure of credit. In love, he has erred by loving not wisely but 'too well', a phrase implying that in following one ideal of passion he has lost sight of another ideal, the particular woman to whom he directed his passion. He recognizes that he has been deceived, 'wrought, Perplexed in the extreme', and he suffers the full pain of having thrown away a pearl richer than all his tribe, whose full worth he can once again appreciate. But rather than presenting these explanations as a form of mitigation of his sins, he accepts the burden of his guiltiness, and by committing suicide he is not necessarily taking an easy way out. 'Let it go all' (v.ii.248) is his simple renunciation of life. He has at least learned something from Desdemona's self-sacrificial interpretation of her own death, and presumably the dramatist trusts that we too have taken the lesson.

Iago also ends the play 'in character'. He has succeeded in, and even surpassed his plans to disrupt a love relationship and upset Othello's peace of mind, and we cannot expect a mere 'accident' of exposure to wring from such a hardened rationalist any kind of apology or show of repentance. He will recognize no concept of poetic justice when he has led his life on a directly opposite principle:

> Work on,
> My medicine work. Thus credulous fools are caught;
> And many worthy and chaste dames even thus,
> All guiltless, meet reproach. What ho!
> (IV.i.44–7)

Accepting no moral sanctions, and living by a creed of opportunism and social demands, he is consistent in his final words:

> Demand me nothing. What you know, you know.
> From this time forth I never will speak word.
> (v.ii.306–7)

The words should be chilling to an audience, for his intimate, buttonholing mode of address, taking us into his confidence during the action, has appealed to the rational, 'plotting' and calculating part of our own minds, eating into our profoundly felt, but sub-rational, sense of injustice. 'What you know, you know' is a threat to any ideals we may hold, for knowledge, and collusion with such a confirmed rationalist, may lead us into a contemptuous or cynical attitude, the 'extreme obduracy of heart' which Keats condemned in Byron,[12] towards anybody who is so fond and foolish as to hold beliefs or moral scruples. The worst thing about Iago is that he *survives*, just as the blatant beast of slander in Book VI of *The Faerie Queene* is still on the loose in society.[13] It would not be surprising if Shakespeare had Spenser in mind in creating this character, for Iago embodies all the rapacious and essentially *social* aspects of the blatant beast. What makes the ending 'almost unbearable' to the person looking for poetic justice or some form of enacted morality, is that Desdemona does not survive. This fact, more even than the death of Othello himself, has led us to question the nature of society not only in the play but, it is to be hoped, in the world.

It is important to remember, although easy to forget, that apart from the first Act, all the action in *Othello* takes place on the sea-coast of Cyprus in and around the citadel. Although Iago speaks knowingly of Venetian customs, all the characters are in fact placed in a kind of enforced solitude as a claustrophobic group in an alien land. Basically, they are living in a military garrison holding uneasy power over a people whose language they almost certainly do not speak. Such circumstances explain much about the atmosphere and moral values held in their community. It is fundamentally a society of men where the soldiers dominate the prevailing attitudes. There are only three women, and the situation by definition places them in a somewhat threatened position, at the mercy of the men. Desdemona is the most central, and because she is young, noble and beautiful she is seen as Woman incarnate. Cassio idolizes her as if she is an angel on a pedestal. Roderigo's feelings are a confused mixture of distant worship and lustful desire to possess her body. Iago, at least deducing from her marriage to Othello that she is a woman of flesh and blood with her own sexual identity, proceeds not on the basis of equality but on the assumption that she is exclusively motivated by her sexuality, and ultimately on the basis that she is, however noble, little more than an object. Othello, cankered by Iago, comes to regard her in the same light and realizes that the only way he can ever truly possess her vitality is by killing it. Given these circumstances and attitudes, one needs little else to explain the tragedy, and amidst it all it is noticeable that no matter what Desdemona does or says herself the attitudes do not change but merely harden. Bianca is a minor victim of male attitudes too. Whether she is a camp-follower or a Cypriot is never explained, but her love for Cassio seems sincere. She is in return exploited by him as a handy sempstress to copy Desdemona's handkerchief and she is spoken of with contempt and dismissiveness by Cassio when he is in male company with Iago:

> *Cassio*: I marry her! What, a customer! I prithee bear some charity to my wit; do not think it so unwholesome. Ha, ha, ha!
>   (IV.i.119–21)

The fact that Othello, overhearing this conversation, can think they are speaking of Desdemona, means that no young woman in love is likely to escape such treatment, given the prevailing attitudes. As he often does with characters of a deprived social class, Shakespeare (and for this we should be grateful) gives her a dignified and self-possessed farewell:

> *Emilia*: Fie, fie upon thee, strumpet!
> *Bianca*: I am no strumpet, but of life as honest
>   As you that thus abuse me.
> *Emilia*: As I! Foh! Fie upon thee!
>   (V.i.121–4)

Bianca, of course, has not accused Emilia of being a strumpet, but we never hear more in retort. Emilia, the third woman in this closed society, presents a more complex case. Having been married to Iago for many years she has evidently learned strategies to survive as a woman, but at times (such as her confrontation with Bianca) she seems ready to adopt her husband's attitudes. Even when speaking to Desdemona in private her general theme is not that men should act differently but that women should emulate them in promiscuity and deceitfulness. She acknowledges that 'it is their husbands' faults If wives do fall' (IV.iii.83–4), but concludes that revenge is sweet and justifies infidelity. The lesson she draws, however, seems soundly enough based:

> And have not we affections,
> Desires for sport, and frailty, as men have?
> Then let them use us well; else let them know
> The ills we do their ills instruct us so.
>   (IV.iii.98–101)

plea for equality in marriage

Her plea, more or less, is for equality in marriage, but she is worldly enough to recognize the existence of a war between the sexes in which the men will not change. Throughout, Emilia acts as a shrewd moral commentator, never taking a high, self-righteous stance, but acting only on the knowledge available to her. Unfortunately, like Desdemona, she is deliberately kept in ignorance of many facts and is prone on occasions to trust her husband. To her credit, when she discovers the deceptions she turns powerfully on her husband, only to be killed. Her final words draw her morally close to Desdemona, as she asks to be laid beside her mistress:

> *Emilia*: What did thy song bode, lady?
> Hark, canst thou hear me? I will play the swan,
> And die in music. [*Sings*] Willow, willow, willow —
> Moor, she was chaste; she lov'd thee, cruel Moor;
> So come my soul to bliss, as I speak true;
> So speaking as I think, alas, I die.
>   (v.ii.249–54)

As an 'experienced victim', Emilia dies in character, speaking her mind, and contributing to the growing consciousness in the audience that a terrible injustice has been perpetrated not just on Desdemona but on women in general.

At this stage in the development of his tragic art, Shakespeare has gone further than in any play towards placing the innocent victim at the very centre of the moral vision, as a touchstone by which to interpret the action. In the 'political' tragedies, *Macbeth*, *Richard III* and *King John*, he has risked the chance of not sufficiently stressing innocence, allowing evil too great a power over our minds to be counteracted by the brief, however powerful, vignettes of the death of children. Perhaps when he wrote the plays this was the jaundiced way in which he saw the world. In *Hamlet*, the general murkiness, dishonesty and obliquity of the society the dramatist is representing has led him to place Ophelia in a rather indirect relationship with the world in which she lives, and although she stirs the greatest pathos, once again Shakespeare may be leaving a little too much to the audience in interpreting the principle of goodness which she represents. He risks no such charges in his depiction of Desdemona. Her fate is presented fully in front of our eyes, on the same level of dramatic interest as the destinies of Othello and Iago, as a damning indictment of specific social and sexual attitudes which are malevolent and which stem directly from complacent and diverse attitudes towards 'justice' and 'poetic justice'. Here he leaves us no excuse for not questioning deeply, with a degree of dismay and anger, the sources of the palpable injustice which we have witnessed. I believe it is not unusual for audiences to feel shocked at the fate of Desdemona (like the first recorded spectator) and it is time that academic criticism recognized and explored this major element of audience response.

VIII Cordelia

When we briefly examined the incident in *King Lear* in which the Servant is killed whilst trying to assist Gloucester, we discovered a pattern of conduct which is repeated by those characters in the play whom we judge as being virtuous. The man's fatal gesture was to stand up against authority, in the person of his own master, in order to assert the dignity of life in the victim, Gloucester. If it be true that 'a dog's obeyed in office', this minor hero refuses to play the game. Earlier, Kent, a trustworthy moral spokesman, has stood up for Cordelia, rather than let an injustice pass:

> Be Kent unmannerly
> When Lear is mad. What wouldst thou do, old man?
> Think'st thou that duty shall have dread to speak
> When power to flattery bows? To plainness honour's bound
> When majesty falls to folly.
> (I.i.144–8)

He is banished for his actions. The Fool is beaten for telling lies and beaten for telling the truth simply because he is in a subservient position, and in order to keep telling the truth he speaks in riddles and allegories which prevent his listeners from pinning him down. Above all, Cordelia provokes the direction of the play by refusing to pay lip-service to the demands of a man who is her father and happens also to be the king. All these characters (including Kent, if we accept his suicidal intention at the end) die as a direct or indirect consequence of actions which demonstrate conscientious civil disobedience against tyrannical exercise of authority. Of these victims, the greatest is Cordelia, and the outrage of readers and audiences resounds over the centuries:

> . . . Shakespeare has suffered the virtue of Cordelia to perish in a just cause, contrary to the natural ideas of justice, to the hope of the reader and, what is yet more strange, to the faith of the chronicles. . . . And if my sensations could add anything to the general suffrage, I might relate, that I was many years ago

shocked by Cordelia's death, that I know not whether I ever endured to read again the last scenes of the play till I undertook to revise them as an editor.[1]

When we ask 'why does Lear die?' we find an answer: he is very old, and in him nature stands at the very verge. When we ask 'why does Lear suffer?' we can answer, with at least partial truth, that he has committed an error of perception against the love and humanity of his daughter, and the loyalty of his best adviser, Kent. It is poetic justice, rationally enforced. But when we ask 'why does Cordelia die?' then echo answers 'Why?' The tragedy is not Lear's. It is Cordelia's. The play is the tragedy *par excellence* of the innocent victim.

The case of Cordelia stands as a paradigm for each of the victims in the play. She simply speaks the truth, rather than saying the words which authority demands and expects of her. Every disaster that occurs in *King Lear* can be traced back eventually to one word, and it is Cordelia's, as she struggles to be truthful to herself. The word is 'Nothing'. Without that word, it is conceivable that she may have become a healthy factor in the balance of power that follows Lear's partition of the kingdom, a force to keep Goneril, Regan and Edmund in check; the king would not have been thrown on the 'hospitality' of his less loving daughters, and would not have suffered the mental anguish of an emotional break with his dearest daughter; and Cordelia herself would not have died in the way she does. Of course, it is possible that evil would have been too powerful under any circumstances, but in the line of dramatic logic, the determining event is Cordelia's word. Given her character, however, the word is inevitable, and it is wrung from her after she shows the greatest reluctance. She first decides upon 'silence', and she is afraid that she may be coerced into using her 'tongue', no matter how dismally she realizes the words will not only be inadequate but will distort the reality. There is only a shadow of a difference between remaining silent and speaking one word, especially when the word is 'nothing', but that shadow-line separates two worlds, in the universe of moral responsibility.

We noticed that Ophelia has inspired much poetry from English writers, and it is invariably the poetry of pity. She is a vulnerable waif, all the more pitiable because she seems oblivious to her own

loneliness, and she draws from the spectator a feeling of protectiveness which is ineffectual because we can watch but never help. It is a
response guided by the yearning sympathy of Gertrude: 'Alas, look
here, my lord' (*Hamlet*, IV.v.35). Cordelia, on the contrary, has
inspired no poetry. She is an awesomely remote figure, confiding no
vulnerability, investing her intimacy only sparingly. We hover
between seeing her as inhuman — a coolly uncompromising truth-
teller, and on the other hand, as non-human — a symbol rather than
a person, embodying other-worldly, spiritual purity. In one sense
Cordelia is a genuine product of the Lear family, maintaining the
independent egotism and resolution of her father and sisters. Otherwise, however, she reveals no emotional needs, and she expresses
her feelings with restraint, enormously expressive in gentle, cradling
rhythms, but often devoid of content or rhetorical amplification:

> Alack, alack!   (IV.vii.40)

> And so I am, I am.   (IV.vii.70)

> No cause, no cause.   (IV.vii.75)

In many ways, the medium of Cordelia's truthfulness is not words,
and it is all the more tragic that she is impaled on a word. We intuit,
through her silence more than her language, that she has feelings of
completely selfless compassion, but she refuses to let us into the
secrets of her emotions. Even her name contains the mystery of the
'heart' of a woman, yoked with the goddess of chastity. She may
herself direct pity towards others, even towards her father who has
wronged her, but she solicits none for herself. Cordelia draws from
us the spellbound respect and wonder that we reserve for the
immortal, or for the work of art, rather than fear and pity for a warm
woman who may die. And so her death leaves us dazed, then
shocked and outraged. Something of a marble permanence, a rock of
truth-telling, is removed and replaced by a limp, dead body in the
arms of a frightened father. It is no wonder that Lear cannot bring
himself to acknowledge that she is dead, and we too are equally
moved and disorientated.

Just as Desdemona has been accused of bringing disaster by telling
lies or by disobeying her father, Cordelia too has no lack of critics.
Some have found error in her initial, dogmatic refusal to reassure
Lear with words as facile as her sisters', on the assumption that

words are easily rendered and cost nothing. The failure to give to a
loving old father the easy answer he wants, to precipitate a chain of
events that will send him mad and make him suffer the extremities of
anguish, is regarded as the action of a spoilt child, petulant because
she must share the rewards with her sisters instead of having them all
to herself. She needs punishment, our stern advocates of filial
gratitude argue, and it is only proper that she should eventually be
the one who kneels for forgiveness. Her most reprehensible fault has
been to degrade 'love' into a matter of duties and obligations, a set of
bargains based upon nothing more than a system of social desert,
rather than emotional needs:

> . . . I love your Majesty
> According to my bond; no more nor less.
> (1.i.91–2)

Love should involve some gratuitous responsiveness to the needs of
another, and as Bottom had said in his rough wisdom, 'to say the
truth, reason and love keep little company together now-a-days'. As
one of Cordelia's milder prosecutors has pointed out, she could learn
a lot about the quality of mercy from one of her literary cousins,
Portia.[2] This is the case against Cordelia, perhaps stated more
strongly than any individual commentator nowadays would put it.
It should be noticed, however, that even to the extreme exponent of
the view, there is a problem in Cordelia's death. If the play is seen in
this way, then there is no need for further punishment after the scene
in which she is forgiven and forgives. Even to the hardest-liner,
death is an excessive revenge from the nemesis of poetic justice.

There are answers to all the criticisms of Cordelia's obstinacy. For
example, it is Lear himself who has introduced the notion that love
involves a large measure of enforced social obligations, for he has
complacently presumed upon his place as a father to demand ex-
pressions of affection as a duty from his daughters, just as later he
uses his position as king to demand obedience from his courtier,
Kent. Beneath the rhetorical charade of apportioning his kingdom
according to verbalizations of devotion, lies a grim and narrow
bargain based on some such implicit statement as 'Recite your
catechism and you will get a reward'. Cordelia is not only breaking
the rules of the game, but also exposing the hollowness of the
exercise, wounding Lear's public pride. Secondly, if it be said that

Cordelia demonstrates unresponsiveness to Lear's needs, then again it is he who has begun the procedure by ignoring the taciturn honesty of her personality. If 'Love is not love Which alters when it alteration finds' (Sonnet 116), then it is a moot point as to who has offended in this case. With her public words, 'Unhappy that I am, I cannot heave My heart into my mouth' (I.i.90–1), Cordelia expresses her own needs. She cannot humiliate herself, or her father, by cheapening an emotion which she sees as properly expressed through actions rather than expedient words. Lear has questioned a relationship by dangerously creating an artificial test of its quality. If Cordelia has betrayed his manifest intentions, then Lear has betrayed her words by making no attempt to understand or respect them. Lear is, fairly consciously, refusing to acknowledge that there may be a meaning deeper than words, whilst Cordelia is equally consciously refusing to provide a rough-and-ready approximation of her feelings in words. For both, the essential problem is the same, based on their respective ideas about love's needs and about the validity of words to grasp and express the meaning of the feelings. In short, the true problem involves words and authority. Lear demands the words as of right, even at the risk that they may be lies: Cordelia will not give the words, simply because they are, of their very nature, lies.

The first scene of *King Lear*, then, certainly shows the failure of words as a means of communication. The more difficult question to answer is whether it also shows a true failure of love. There is a curious but palpable impression even in the heat of their anger, that Lear and his youngest daughter do love each other very much, and that paradoxically they are showing the strength of this love in action. The paradox is that only a person whom Lear loved dearly could draw out the violence of his rage in a scene where he holds virtually ultimate authority (unlike some later scenes, when his anger is displayed in impotence); whilst Cordelia could be so upset and unbending only on an issue which mattered supremely to her emotional life. In fact, the scene may be evidence that, in moments of extremity, the adage that 'Love is not love Which alters when it alteration finds' is true on a deeper level of meaning than meets the eye. In this case, not just one but both participants stand firm on the principle, of inflexible love, for they are both fighting profoundly for their love on personal and temporarily incompatible terms. It is merely speculation, but one suspects that Lear would be capable of disinheriting either Goneril or Regan more perfunctorily and without so much rage, because his relationships with these daughters do not seem so firmly built upon strong, mutual feelings of love. Cordelia's adamant refusal to meet his demands (and when forced, to answer 'wrongly') is not simply a formal irregularity in the procedure. It touches Lear on the quick since it comes from 'our joy, although our last and least', and exposes the irrelevance of the demands when they meet the truth about the nature of love. His self-defence against the pain is anger, in an attempt to deny even to himself the knowledge that he has taken a terrible risk in asking that feelings should be stretched into brazen words. Similarly, Cordelia's actions spring from a profound recognition of the risks. Love should not be coerced, subjected to bullying or authoritarian demands. If it could be slotted into the world of political institutions, it would no longer be love but enforced obedience. The audience has the benefit of her aside, 'I am sure my love's More ponderous than my tongue' (i.i.76–7), but she cannot speak this publicly because even these words would be inadequate to her feelings. Her own unconscious strategy in the situation is a form of civil disobedience based on passive non-co-operation. She follows up an apparently empty and impertinent 'Nothing' with a rational but rebellious reference to social duties and obligations. The significance of her gesture may be stated in this way. She acts out the philosophy that 'love' should not be used to justify tyranny. Hers is the raw and disturbing voice that asserts that no relationship is worth losing faith with oneself, for to do so would be to negate love itself. She refuses to accept the tyranny of authority for its own sake in an emotional field, just as Kent refuses in the political sphere. But these lessons are not immediately learned by Lear.

There is in this scene something very close to the lovers' quarrels in *Antony and Cleopatra*: simply because they love each other so much, neither partner can afford to reveal the pain that only the other can inflict, and they take refuge in verbal flanking movements of rage and non-co-operation respectively. In the volatile first scene, most of Lear's emotional attention is directed towards his youngest daughter, and all of Cordelia's love is focused upon her father. Although the issue of love is rooted in the family rather than in a sexual relationship, it is no less intense for that. The confrontation is an almost impossible test of the feelings within the characters. To speak of 'misunderstanding' is somehow wrong, for we get the impression that they do not actually misunderstand each other. Rather, communication, based upon mutual access to a common understanding and shared vocabulary, is deliberately withheld on both sides, because the public occasion demands a form of language too crudely inflexible to bear the weight of private feelings. Words may be appropriate to express love under some conditions, but not within the scenario prepared by Lear, which is a political occasion taking its nature from the central admission and imposition of authority. Under such constraints, words may be used to threaten or to tell expedient, politically motivated lies, but not 'feelingly' to express the truth of the emotions. It is the failing of other characters in the play not to distinguish between the two uses of language. The other father, Gloucester, chooses to trust the politically motivated words of Edmund, rather than seeking for the truth, and in doing so he commits Lear's error.

Since much of the action takes place under conditions in which people may be damned for their words rather than their feelings, Cordelia is consistently seen as a prototype victim of her society. Lacking 'that glib and oily art To speak and purpose not' (I.i.224–5), her attempts to communicate, though doomed to futility, operate in a different, and often non-verbal medium. She has 'heavenly eyes' (IV.iii.30), and this becomes an emblem for her own truth-telling. She leaves the court 'with washed eyes' (I.i.268), and later we have the moving report of her sorrow, described in visual terms, like a tableau: 'an ample tear trill'd down Her delicate cheek':

> You have seen
> Sunshine and rain at once; her smiles and tears
> Were like a better way. Those happy smilets
> That play'd on her ripe lip seem'd not to know
> What guests were in her eyes, which parted thence
> As pearls from diamonds dropp'd. In brief,
> Sorrow would be a rarity most beloved
> If all could so become it.
>   (IV.iii.12–3 and 17–24)

Her appearance is expressive of a meaning that lies otherwise dumb,

but rather than translate it into words, she breathes only broken
snatches:

> Faith, once or twice she heav'd the name of father
> Pantingly forth, as if it press'd her heart;
> Cried 'Sisters! sisters! Shame of ladies! Sisters!
> Kent! father! sisters! What i'th'storm? i'th'night?
> Let pity not be believ'd!' There she shook
> The holy water from her heavenly eyes,
> And clamour moisten'd; then away she started
> To deal with grief alone.
> (IV.iii.25–32)

With the reappearance of Cordelia herself, we have confirmation
that eyes may be a more trustworthy index of truth than words,
although the words here are more blessed than any that have gone
before:

> All blest secrets,
> All you unpublish'd virtues of the earth,
> Spring with my tears; be aidant and remediate,
> In the good man's distress.
> (IV.iv.15–18)

Unlike the other characters who make invocations, she is not
praying to external gods or powers such as fortune, but to something inward; human virtues which in their 'unpublish'd' secrecy
hold a mysterious silence.[3] Her 'mourning and importun'd tears'
spring from an intuitive source of virtuous understanding, and they
'publish' a meaning to the sympathetic witness more directly than
her words.

Before the father may be reconciled with his daughter, he must
learn the falsity of his own advice when he says to the blind
Gloucester, 'A man may see how this world goes with no eyes. Look
with thine ears' (IV.vi.150–1). The error committed by both old
men has been to trust their ears before their eyes and hearts, without
recognizing that words can easily be formed into lies and half-truths.
The tragedy for both is that their respective reconciliations with son
and daughter, the 'blessings' afforded them, come too late for any
sustained tranquillity or relationship.[4]

The reconciliation between Lear and Cordelia is one of the most moving scenes in all literature, because so much is happening beneath the words. Inexpressible tenderness is conveyed on both sides in reticent understatement. The moments have a hushed and reverent economy. The scene opens with the re-meeting of the two plain speakers, Cordelia and Kent, who have communicated with each other in letters, preparing for this very scene. Cordelia, who has consistently demonstrated a belief that truth should be openly revealed for all to see, exhorts Kent to discard his disguise and to appear in his own person. Kent, having observed the dangers involved in being too open at court, cautiously prefers to remain unobserved until he is quite sure that the right moment has come for his self-revelation. It is interesting that Edgar too remains disguised until after he needs to, and their actions show that they have both bitterly learned a political lesson from their experiences. It is necessary at court to hold something back and employ strategic subterfuges, disguises and lies in order to survive. Cordelia, in contrast, has resisted the lesson of expedience, and almost as a direct consequence she does not survive. It cannot be held against her that she is so consistent and integrated in her beliefs. The result can instead be turned against her society. Her point to Kent is that it would be more gracious and gentle to the King if all 'memories of those worser hours' could be blotted out. She reveals her own desire in the simple restraint of her address to Lear when he awakens:

> How does my royal lord? How fares your majesty?
> (IV.vii.44)

Here she is compromising her stubborn refusal to recognize authority, although characteristically her sympathy and compassion is the reason for her form of address. In her words she extends to him the full dignity of his former office as king, rather than father. Tactful, deferential, and outwardly without pity or self-pity, she refrains from any reference to darker times in the past. His own lacerated memory, however, impinges on the present moment. 'Bound upon a wheel of fire' his tears 'Do scald like molten lead' (IV.vii.46–8). Tears from his interior feelings have come to punish him from the outside, and the mental sufferings of the tragic hero are upon him. But under her soothing hand, he is able to recognize himself and his daughter, as if the tears have washed his eyes clean:

> Pray, do not mock me:
> I am a very foolish fond old man,
> Four score and upward, not an hour more or less;
> And, to deal plainly,
> I fear I am not in my perfect mind.
>   . . .
> Do not laugh at me;
> For, as I am a man, I think this lady
> To be my child Cordelia.
>   (IV.vii.59–70)

In a moment of full and beautiful clarity, he sees that she is not laughing: 'Be your tears wet?' (IV.vii.71). It is a statement from a wondering world of fingertip touch, breaking through all the barriers that the misuse of words has placed between people, revealing as much of the truth as his earlier, wordy fulminations had concealed. In this scene, hushed as a little chapel, words become true indexes of feeling: words of prayer and hymn, words of quiet understatement, and words that simply describe tactile sensation: 'Be your tears wet?' Cordelia can co-operate with Lear now, for his language is not a weapon of authoritarian control, but a medium for honest thought, reflection, and true communication.

Before moving on to the ending of the play, we may linger a while in the company of the Fool for his situation exemplifies various aspects of the dangers of authority and of language when it is used to coerce others. Although many people in the play take exception to his words and threaten him with punishment for his impertinent speech, his professional position exempts him from facing the full consequences of what he says. It is his role to turn the world upside down, to insult rather than to flatter, to say whatever he wishes instead of what he 'ought' to say, or is told to say, and so he can speak unpleasant truths without invoking the full penalty invited by Cordelia in her own social circumstances. The Fool has a licence to be anti-authoritarian, and his language reveals this stance in different ways. His mode of speech is so gnomic and oblique, so whimsically individual, that nobody actually seems to understand him immediately. Many realize that he is insulting or criticizing them, but because they comprehend his tone and not often his meanings which are delivered in a private code, they cannot respond immediately. He is, in fact, protected not only by his privileged position, but by his very language, which holds in itself a form of disobedient resistance to the bullying of others. However, the reader (if not the audience in the theatre), has time to examine his words, tease out their meanings, and eventually acknowledge his superior insight into truth. He sees through every moral error, he punctures every illusion and pomposity, penetrates every disguise, and interprets the form of reasoning that lies behind Lear's 'mad' statements.[5] The Fool, then, in many ways is very close to Cordelia, but for reasons of social role and mode of language, he is both more protected than she, and more ineffectual.

The Fool is also allowed by the dramatist to take up the option of total silence, which was Cordelia's first choice but which she was not allowed to implement. He simply drops out of the vocabulary of the play, into utter silence. With his usual, uncanny precision, he forecasts his silence in his last words: 'And I'll go to bed at noon' (III.vi.85). From this noonday point in the play (at a time when the illusion of the action is that it is a naughty night), he sleeps out the rest. He has been following Cordelia from the outset, not only in practising her principle of not speaking except when the truth may be told, but also in a more yearning, emotionally loyal way: 'Since my young lady's going into France, sir, the Fool hath much pined away' (I.iv.72). Now he has demonstrated her own understanding that language itself is useless when nobody will listen to the truth. He has often voiced the paradoxes and punishments involved in plain talk:

> I marvel what kin thou and thy daughters are. They'll have me whipp'd for speaking true; thou'lt have me whipp'd for lying; and sometimes I am whipp'd for holding my peace.
> (I.iv.180–3)

The Fool is describing the predicament faced by each of the virtuous characters in the play, Cordelia, Kent and Edgar. Just as they are forced to adopt a disguise (or in the case of Cordelia, to go underground), so he is forced to mask his words in hieroglyphics, and eventually to disappear into silence. The predicament for each is created by the demands made by other characters, revealed most clearly in their use of language as a form of coercive tyranny. At least by the very end of the play, an element of the lesson has been learned and the order has been somewhat changed: 'Speak what we feel, not what we ought to say' (v.iii.324). This change for the better is one healthy consequence of the death of Cordelia, a representative standing for all the victims in the play, and if so then she has not died entirely in vain.

However terrible the ending of *King Lear*, it presents us with a triumph of seeing and plain-speaking, as the play's world is sobered into a recognition of what it has ignored and covered up, until the removal of Cordelia's life. Lear's words as he enters with his daughter's body are full of expressiveness and emotional truth, as he turns his impotent grief into active rage by blaming the world for its indifference:

> Howl, howl, howl, howl! O, you are men of stones!
> Had I your tongues and eyes, I'd use them so
> That heaven's vault should crack. She's gone for ever!
> (v.iii.257–9)

He demands the use of tongues and eyes, not to tell political lies and disguise the truth in illusions, but to cry rejection of a world that allows the occurrence of such injustices as are now in front of us. Here we have the dramatist placing the body of the innocent victim right at the centre of our gaze, demanding our responses through vision, feeling and verbalized anger. The unbearable fact of the ending to this play is that Shakespeare has taken his victim from the hands of her persecutors, and rather than distracting us with the world's rationalizations and with the male protagonist's self-recriminating suffering, has relentlessly forced his characters and his audience to concentrate wholly upon the injustice. He could have done so in *Titus Andronicus*, *Hamlet*, *Othello* and the other plays, but there he has given the world the last say, in order to restore some part of our complacent assumption that the suffering hero, and the social fabric, are more important than the regrettable death of an innocent. The words that ring through this scene, which is full of outwardly directed anger and powerfully expressed feelings of outrage, are Albany's 'O, see, see' and Lear's

> Look on her. Look, her lips,
> Look there, look there!
> (v.iii.310–11)

The relatively minor suffering of the disguised Kent is relegated to a
lower level of importance, and his revelation of identity, carefully
prepared as a theatrical denouement, is brushed aside in Lear's
off-hand recognition and his 'I'll see that straight' (v.iii.287).
Edgar's successful revenge of his father's death and his own honour
is similarly forgotten, in the absolute concentration upon the victim,
unprecedented in Shakespeare's plays:

> I know when one is dead and when one lives;
> She's dead as earth.
> (v.iii.260)

The death of the villain, Edmund, is counted 'but a trifle here'
(v.iii.296). We are not allowed to escape the sight of the body and its
significance. When Albany, acting on the assumption that the king
and the play are virtually finished, proceeds to the practical arrange-
ments for the future and the apportionment of poetic justice, rewards for the virtuous, punishment for the wicked, he is suddenly
arrested by a cry that condemns the society which has consistently
forgotten the price paid for its political equilibrium:

> *Lear*: And my poor fool is hang'd! No, no, no life!
> Why should a dog, a horse, a rat, have life,
> And thou no breath at all? Thou'lt come no more,
> Never, never, never, never, never!
> (v.iii.305–7)

Whether we take it that Lear is referring to Cordelia or his professional Fool is not a question we can answer, although it is significant
that we can even ask the question.[6] Pre-eminently they are both
innocent victims of a society which believes in authoritarian coercion and in using words as a way of creating expedient illusions and
lies, rather than as a medium for truth. They have both been
forgotten several times by the play's world and the audience, and
rather than risk letting the point slip by, the dramatist relentlessly
places it time and again before our eyes. The sight of Cordelia's dead
body brings back to us all that has been forgotten in the heat of a

moment. The Servant's brave action was forgotten; the Fool no longer exists to the play's world; Cordelia died 'accidentally', whilst everybody forgot her, engrossed as they were in the chivalric pomp and ceremony of Edgar's avenging joust with his brother: 'Great thing of us forgot!' (v.iii.236). All has been a forgetting until it is too late, and for this the world is responsible and specifically at fault. This time Shakespeare gives us no pretty words of pity from Gertrude; no martyr's action from the victim. He gives us simply the sight itself, lest we too forget. After the death of Lear, there is a feeling amongst the spectators on stage of muted, shamed quietness, a response which seems the only one possible after such sustained outrage perpetrated against justice and fairness. 'A plague upon you, murderers, traitors all!' (v.iii.269) cries Lear, forgetting that he too has been one in this interlude. If the moral heart of the play is to beat in our minds, we should not cherish too much our compassion for the suffering Lear, converting 'catharsis' into a justification for self-indulgence. Better to contemplate with sorrow and anger the events which killed his loving daughter, for in such events as these we are all implicated.

A view of the play which takes Lear himself as the centre leads inevitably to the issues and themes which generations of critics have toiled over: whether a king should abdicate, what his proper responsibilities are towards his subjects, the nature of extreme mental suffering and, more personally, topics like Lear's 'madness', his 'moral enlightenment' and his spiritual development considered parallel to the other old character, Gloucester. By taking a consistent line of concern for Cordelia (and her qualities which are embodied in other characters) we find ourselves reversing priorities in a way which, although initially it appears to take a fish's eye view of *King Lear*, in fact opens up new and profoundly important issues: the justifications and consequences of civil disobedience, the morally questionable nature of power itself, the ultimate effectiveness of an expression of conscience and principle in a political context, the sources of violence when met by pacifism, and many others. By raising such questions we widen the scope of the ways in which we interpret the action, and such an exercise may eventually provide more adequate reasons for explaining the play's undoubted power and comprehensiveness of tragic vision. Lear's own mind leads us up against a baffled, metaphysical boundary beyond which we cannot go except with the platitudes of Edgar and Albany. Cordelia's *actions*, however, and their consequences, lead us outwards into genuine problems of a person's place in a social and political context, problems which can be debated openly, 'demystified' without losing the essential mystery of how a single mind can create such a searching work, and perhaps can even be resolved. This is the least defeatist, most positive and healthy response to the question 'Why does Cordelia die?' It is a course which is itself Cordelia-like, for she has shown us the way to question and resist authority. It is finally her sheer strength of will that marks a development in Shakespeare's presentation of this sort of character, for Cordelia refuses to accept the situational helplessness which is the undoing of Lucrece, Ophelia and Desdemona. At this stage, he can show us that innocence does not mean weakness.

IX After Thoughts

In this brief book, I have not attempted to be thorough, for the subject itself would baffle such an attempt. Instead, I have tried to establish certain general priorities which should have a place in the way we think and talk about Shakespearean tragedy. There is in each tragedy an innocent victim who is accorded neither justice in her own world, nor poetic justice in the work of art. This is not a mistake made by Shakespeare, nor is it an immoral action on his part, for the function of the victims is to awaken our moral imaginations to the existence of injustice, and to train our own moral faculties. The victim stands as a model of goodness by which to judge the relative flaws in those around, including the tragic 'hero'. The exact nature of the victim's role is unique to the world of each play, and requires separate and sensitive exploration. It is perhaps in the nature of the concept of injustice that it involves specific unfairness to an individual, whereas a state of justice is a more collective notion, depending upon equal rights for all within a group. It may follow also that our recognition of injustice is primarily through the imaginative awareness of an individual's suffering, whilst justice is seen to be rational, reasonable, and utilitarian.[1] For these reasons, the subject condemns one to arguing for the validity of knowledge acquired through the imagination, and to discussing examples of injustice in a pragmatic, individual context. To argue for either of these positions is not an easy task since there is an overwhelming and usually unstated orthodoxy directing us to assume that knowledge is rationality while justice is determined by what is acceptable to a majority. It is perhaps the ingrained nature of these assumptions in our culture which explains why Shakespeare's treatment of the innocent victim has fallen on stony ground.

The subject is interesting for formal as well as moral reasons. Shakespeare innovated and was remarkably consistent in using in his tragedies an inset plot demonstrating victimization within an overarching, dominant plot concerned with the 'great man'. The significance of the former is primarily to awaken our emotional and moral responses. The main effects may be to allow us to question and distance ourselves from the tragic hero, to turn our eyes away from 'characterization' as a self-justifying end in itself, and to make us aware of the play as a presentation of ideas, conflicts and moral predicaments all of which are larger and more abiding than the individual. Viewed in this light, Shakespeare's structural and ethical thoughtfulness become all the more impressive and interrelated. Very few writers have chosen or dared to emulate such a feat. One can see signs of the attempt in the novels of Tolstoy and, more insistently, Dostoyevsky. Perhaps one could cite *Bleak House* (littered with victims of the law) and *The Mayor of Casterbridge* as English examples. A more prevalent practice, however, is to follow one structure or the other rather than retaining sympathy on both levels. Thus we have plays and novels based on *either* 'the protagonist as victim' *or* 'the victim as protagonist'. It is interesting that Shakespeare's immediate successor, Webster, employs both kinds of tragedy in his two most celebrated plays. In *The White Devil* Vittoria is presented as wicked, but at various points (especially in the trial scene), Webster makes us clearly aware that her evil is a strategy for survival in the hypocritical and duplicitous social world of the court. Webster is in a calculated way drawing our attention away from the character's 'aberrant' psychological makeup and forcing us to recognize the existence of evil in society itself. In *The Duchess of Malfi* he gives us a Shakespearean victim, innocent, dignified and isolated, again in order to activate our moral responses to question and condemn the social evil in her world. The significant difference from Shakespeare's practice is that, although Webster kills off the Duchess in the middle of the play he does not allow the possibility of the audience pinning its sympathies upon a dominant character. One might think Webster is either less subtle or more morally ingenuous than Shakespeare, who runs the risk of demanding too much of an audience in retaining some sympathy for the hero even after undercutting him. Whatever the reason, Webster has had enough followers to claim him as the rightful head of a whole genre unequivocally celebrating the victim. To name only more obvious examples we have Richardson's *Clarissa*, Hardy's *Tess of the D'Urbervilles* and *Jude the Obscure*, Ellison's *The Invisible Man* and perhaps Salinger's *The Catcher in the Rye*. Other art forms have used the victim to potent effect. We recall the anguished faces on Goya's man about to be executed and on the horse at the centre of Picasso's *Guernica*. On

American film there are many modern examples, from Monroe in *The Misfits*, who monitors the existence of cruelty rather than centrally being the victim herself, to Dustin Hoffman in *Midnight Cowboy*. These examples may be accepted as masterpieces, but the multitude of others in the field alerts us to the inbuilt danger of the mode: its proximity to sentimentality. Sentiment may be a healthy force to call into being when one wants to clarify some social evil, but sentiment for its own sake becomes a meaningless diversion from the exercise of the moral faculty. Shakespeare's more complex method may run the risk of allowing the hardhearted to ignore the existence of the innocent victim, but it never falls prey to the charge of gratuitous sentimentality.

It is possible that this book has given its readers no fresh insight into the detail of Shakespeare's plays (although naturally I hope it has), but a more worthwhile result of the book would be if it helps to change the nature of the debate about tragedy. We have been analysing the heroes for long enough, denying a place of influence for the victims, simply because they do not have the worldly power to put their cases eloquently. There are signs of gradual change, as critics ask new questions. A recent book on the subject, John Bayley's *Shakespeare and Tragedy*[2] is marked by a tentativeness of tone and humility of attitude, and it begins at least to judge the action partly from a knowledge of the centrality of characters such as Desdemona and Cordelia. We can begin now to appreciate the 'totality' of each play not as an intricate, intellectual jig-saw puzzle, built around the picture of a great man, but as the complexity of an imaginative and emotional experience which demands a fully awakened moral responsiveness. In other words, criticism can at last duplicate the immediacy of impression and judgment which audiences in the theatre find straightforward, instinctive and natural.

Appendix: Critics and Victims

I have two aims in this section: first, to show that critics are inclined to be hard on 'victims' in Shakespeare's tragedies, and secondly to examine some of the tacit assumptions that lie behind the harsh attitudes.

Let us take two examples, chosen almost at random although from influential commentators. These statements are not particularly significant in themselves, but they are symptomatic of a general tendency amongst critics. Nicholas Brooke, in his sound and very useful book *Shakespeare's Early Tragedies*, referring twice to the 'embarrassment' of Lavinia's presence in *Titus Andronicus*, comments on a passage in this way:

> As in Act I, effective use is made of surprise. The 'gentle' Lavinia enters with her husband and taunts Tamora for her lust:
> 'Tis thought you have a goodly gift in horning,
> And to be doubted that your Moor and you
> Are singled forth to try experiments.
> (II.iii.67–9)

The vulgarity of tone is at once cheap, stupid, and dangerous. It is as unexpected as Lucius-the-Roman's barbarity in Act I. And it is as convincing: it would be sentimental indeed to look for a nice little heroine in this play. Lavinia, here, has the beastliness of a conscious virtue, and her vindictiveness anticipates the later action. She is to be dumb and helpless, and careless *readers* may therefore forget her presence in later Acts; but she is, like Ovid's Philomel, to be *active* in the vile revenge. Even in Lavinia, the paradise garden is also a barren detested vale.[1]

Does Lavinia really deserve the rejectiveness of such a tone? Even if we grant that her own three lines are spirited to the point of pertness, we need not see them as 'cheap, stupid, and dangerous', for in the situation she has no clues about what is to follow. She cannot adjust her tone in the knowledge of foresight, as the critic may. And what is the meaning of the curious phrase, 'the beastliness of conscious virtue'? To put the question more pertinently, does Lavinia's fully justified accusation of Tamora automatically qualify her for rape, dismemberment and eventual murder? It would seem, to say the least, a little easier to suggest that Lavinia's 'conscious virtue' is important to the moral design of the whole play, just as her later helplessness (as Brooke points out but does not emphasize or follow up) is also crucial. Her presence in many different ways prevents us adopting a point of view which may prostitute the horrors of the play to mere entertainment. She is radically different in her role from the rest of the characters, placed in order to set a moral check upon the audience's acceptance of the brutality of the revenge ethic pursued by her society. One can easily see why the critic should wish to taint her with the beastliness, for it fits neatly his attempt to find aesthetic unity in the play, based on the premise that 'they are all alike', and his explication of the theme as 'the emergence of the beast in man'.[2] The desire to implicate Lavinia in such a blunt and unjustified way is, sadly, unnecessary. The point about 'the beastliness of man' (or as I have argued, the perniciousness of a particular moral dogma held by this society, the revenge ethic), could be proved more powerfully and effectively, without introducing the uneasy proposition that the audience is *always* judging the play with 'judicial detachment', and that it is *always* emotionally un-involved in the action, if we were to accept fully the terrible victimization of Lavinia as central, and as a touchstone governing our moral sympathies. Such a position does not involve us in springing earnestly upon three unguarded and morally acute lines spoken by the character early in the play, and painting them in the darkest possible colours.

My second example illustrates the same critical tendency. Clifford Leech, an important and often inspiring critic, points out in an essay the difference of language between Desdemona and Emilia, but what he chooses to make of the difference is again excessively hard on Desdemona:

> . . . The contrast is pointed by Emilia's speaking in prose, Desdemona in blank verse:
> *Desdemona:* Dost thou in conscience think, tell me, Emilia,
>   That there be women do abuse their husbands
>   In such gross kind?

Emilia: There be some such, no question.
Desdemona: Wouldst thou do such a deed for all the world?
Emilia: Why, would not you?
Desdemona: No, by this heavenly light!
Emilia: Nor I, neither by this heavenly light; I might do't as well
    i'th' dark.
Desdemona: Wouldst thou do such a deed for all the world?
Emilia: The world is a huge thing; 'tis a great price for a small vice.
Desdemona: In troth, I think thou wouldst not.
Emilia: In troth, I think I should, and undo't when I had done.
    Marry, I would not do such a thing for a joint-ring, nor
    for measures of lawn, nor for gowns, petticoats, nor caps,
    nor any petty exhibition; but for the whole world, — why,
    who would not make her husband a cuckold to make him a
    monarch? I should venture purgatory for it.
Desdemona: Beshrew me, if I would do such a wrong
    For the whole world.
Emilia: Why, the wrong is but a wrong i'th'world; and having the
    world for your labour, 'tis a wrong in your own world,
    and you might quickly make it right.
Desdemona: I do not think there is any such woman.
    (IV.iii.77–82)

The passage makes us see Desdemona's capacity for self-deception, for Brabantio had kept her in no cloister, and perhaps we begin to wonder too if this woman's conscious virtue is after all so admirable a thing. Does it not depend, we may ask, on a deliberate blindness to the common ways of human nature, and is there not a touch of complacency here – for even Desdemona does not pretend that men are so faithful as she claims women to be.[3]

Frankly, there is so much wrong with this comment that it is hard to know quite where to start. It should be recognized first that in the passage quoted, Desdemona consistently adopts a deeply serious tone, trying to make Emilia speak equally seriously. She is denied the chance since Emilia consistently adopts a jocular, bawdy tone, unaware of the terror, bewilderment and incomprehension Desdemona must be feeling at this moment, faced with the erratic and obsessive behaviour of her husband. Desdemona is more starkly isolated than ever in this scene, for even a female confidante will not take seriously her greatest worry. Secondly, reduced by the non-responsiveness of Emilia to mere repetition, all that Desdemona actually says is that *she* cannot be unfaithful, and because she feels this so strongly, she cannot comprehend how other women can be faithless to a husband. This sentiment is perfectly in character with everything else she has said throughout the play, and perhaps it is consistent with what any newly-wed marriage partner, male or female, would say at the time, for otherwise there would be no point in marriage. Thirdly, it is remarkable how close the words and philosophy used by Emilia are to the statements of her husband, which were quoted on page 82. She is not necessarily speaking as a woman, but as the conditioned mouthpiece of Iago, which makes Desdemona's 'I do not think there is any such woman' extremely functional, paralleling her own 'these men, these men', and standing in tacit opposition in the design of the play to Iago's 'Be a man'. Now, for the critic. Does the 'self-deception' reside in the frightened and serious Desdemona, or in the flippant Emilia? It is at least an open question. What is the relevance of Desdemona's father not keeping her 'in a cloister'? Experience of the world need not of itself mean an absence of deep moral conviction which allows the woman to say 'I would not do such a thing'. What is so wrong with 'this woman's conscious virtue' (a phrase which, curiously and accidentally, occurred in Brooke's comment), when it is so patently consistent and heartfelt? What exactly are the 'common ways of human nature' which Leech feels so confident that Desdemona, presumably consciously, is denying, whilst he knows them all with, dare one say, 'a touch of complacency'? (In fact, his last sentence implies that Desdemona *does* know something of male attitudes; is it not more sensitive to say then that she has made a firm moral decision, rather than accusing her of 'self-deception'?) It is clear, reading between the lines, that the critic has tacitly accepted the morality proposed by Emilia (or, as I would say, Iago), as the *correct* code. He has done so in order to prove a more general thematic preoccupation in the play upon 'self-deception'. But why tar with the same brush the very character who stands against the Iago vision, and against self-deception, when it is her presence and firmness which stand as a touchstone for us to judge the conscious immorality of others? In short, what is happening here is that, just as Iago thought he spotted in Desdemona a potentially fickle, knowing, promiscuous and sensual woman, so has the critic. And yet if we should accept for a moment such a stance, how can we possibly believe that Desdemona is fully, consistently and sincerely faithful to Othello in every word she says and in every action: in other words, how can we believe in what the play so obviously and patently requires us to believe in?

It would be tedious and unnecessary to enumerate more examples of individual critics' momentary lapses into demeaning the role of the virtuous victim. Instead, let us turn to the attitudes that lie behind the general critical failure to deal with the subject.

As usual when raising questions of Shakespearean interpretation, we cannot do better than begin with Dr Johnson. Observing strictly the laws of poetic justice, he finds fault with Shakespeare:

> His first defect is that to which may be imputed most of the evil in books or in men. He sacrifices virtue to convenience, and is so much more careful to please than to instruct, that he seems to write without any moral purpose. From his writings indeed a system of social duty may be selected, for he that thinks reasonably must think morally; but his precepts and axioms drop casually from him; he makes no just distribution of good or evil, nor is always careful to shew in the virtuous a disapprobation of the wicked; he carries his persons indifferently through right and wrong, and at the close dismisses them without further care, and leaves their examples to operate by chance. This fault the barbarity of his age cannot extenuate; for it is always a writer's duty to make the world better, and justice is a virtue independent on time or place.[4]

Since the argument of the present book has been that Shakespeare does not forfeit the writer's duty to 'make the world better', I hope that no more detail is necessary at this stage. The interest now lies in what Johnson is ignoring in making this statement. It is interesting that his attack on Shakespeare takes the opposite starting-point from that of modern critics, to whom we shall soon turn. Whilst the latter take the moral line that 'evil is necessary' and therefore that there must be victims, Johnson believes optimistically that evil is unnecessary, and that literature is an instrument for condemning it. What he leaves out of his scheme, however, is the existence of the feelings and moral imagination in audiences and readers, which Shakespeare works hard upon, so that we can be stirred to a moral attitude by recognizing and sympathizing with the plight of victims. By requiring the dramatist to make his moral system explicit and universally applicable like a set of rules, 'independent on time or place', Johnson is neglecting the operation of an audience's or reader's moral imagination which, without being told, can be stirred to admiration or outrage by a particular example of virtue or vice. As a stark example, it can confidently be said that an audience will immediately realize that the blinding of Gloucester is an appallingly wicked act, that the Servant's gesture is a brave and good one and for this understanding we need no elaborate choric spokesman. It can safely be left to 'operate by chance' because in the audience as in the dramatist, 'he that thinks reasonably must think morally'. We are judging intuitively and emotionally the moral nature of situations, at virtually all points of a dramatic piece. The 'instruction' we receive from such a moment, concerning the nature of cruelty and coercion, is no less real, and perhaps more powerful, for the fact that the dramatist leaves us to draw the lesson. D.H. Lawrence, for one, has warned us that if a writer himself 'puts his finger on the balance' and tells us what to think about an incident in his work, he runs the risk of deadening the true moral import, of bullying us into acceptance of a programmed moral code, rather than leaving us to learn for ourselves.[5] For an illustration, we need only contemplate for a moment the eighteenth century's attempts to 'clean up' Shakespeare's morality. Nahum Tate, by giving a happy ending to *King Lear* was exonerating the play of potential misreading and misunderstanding, but at the cost of making the 'moral' too complacent to be felt keenly. How much more effective in raising the outrage and proper moral sympathies of generations of audiences, readers, and even sometimes critics, is Shakespeare's own ending!

Modern criticism is no less guilty than Johnson of ignoring the autonomy and integrity — even the existence — of the moral imagination, although the reasons are almost the reverse. Determinded not to be prescriptive or dogmatic, twentieth-century critics find it fashionable to reject altogether the possibility that we are compelled by the plays to make judgments about the action. Convinced that evil is inevitable and necessary, that the world is too complex for an individual to make any sense of it, or that it is arrogant to maintain rigorous moral principles, they insist on an agnosticism based on the belief that Shakespeare, because he takes Iago and Edmund as seriously (in the psychological sense) as virtuous characters, is allowing us to make no distinction between vice and virtue. The text for such a position is often given in the form of a misreading of Keats's famous comment on the 'poetical Character':

. . . it is not itself — it has no self — it is every thing and nothing. It has no character — it enjoys light and shade; it lives in gusto, be it foul or fair, high or low, rich or poor, mean or elevated — It has as much delight in conceiving an Iago as an Imogen. What shocks the virtuous philosopher delights the camelion Poet. It does no harm from its relish of the dark side of things any more than from its taste for the bright one; because they both end in speculation.[6]

In the light of Keats's other comments on Shakespeare and his own repeated desire to 'do the world some good', it is inconceivable that Keats would knowingly wish to say that the dramatist in his plays is not teaching us something about right and wrong, simply because he takes all characters equally seriously, in a democratic and republican fashion. The crucial word is 'speculation', which always in Keats holds a powerful moral content. The dramatist would be unwise to pretend that evil does not exist in the world, but he would be immoral to pretend that it is just as acceptable and valid as virtue. His duty is not only to show us villainy in action, in some credible detail, but also to show us that it should be noticed, and its effects analysed, isolated and condemned. Taken in the context of Keats's letter, and his other writings as a whole, his comment does not reject the instructive powers of literature, for it is this that he most constantly reiterates. Rather, he is explaining through the example of Shakespeare's characters that 'axioms are not axioms until they are proved upon our pulses', and that literature may be just as valid an experience, if the moral imagination is exercised, as any other parts of our existence. Another implication of the comment is that 'good' and 'evil' may be relative to a particular time and situation. The rich man, the church, a government may condemn as evil what our own imaginations tell us is not so in the moral conditions imposed by a moment; whereas the poor man, the rebel, or the ordinary citizen may well think from time to time that every action taken by authority will not inevitably be right and moral. Simply because a crude and explicit 'moral' is not appended to certain situations in Shakespeare does not mean that we are not compelled to take a moral attitude towards them, for the axiom may be proved upon the pulses of our imaginative experience. Once morality is taken to include the mysterious workings of the imagination, the poet's medium *par excellence* and the quality which Keats at least never forgets, then we can grasp at once both the wrongness of Johnson's belief in an absolute moral code, 'independent on time or place', and also the limitations of a more modern assumption that there is no implicit moral perspective awakened in watching a tragedy.

A.C. Bradley, in his wonderful book, *Shakespearean Tragedy*, sets the tone for the modern agnosticism, although he is never so crude in its application as his professional successors. He is fully aware of the problems. Time and again, Bradley delicately describes our own distress and pain when watching the plight of Shakespeare's tragic women, but he gives only description rather than analysis, baulking at a rigorous examination of the implications of events which caused the deaths. Presumably, such an exploration would place the tragic hero here in a lesser light, and so the victims are carefully kept apart, lest the whole enterprise of examining the tragic hero's suffering be endangered. The procedure is admirably consistent with Bradley's constant assertion, surely based on acceptance of the Christian adage, 'judge not lest ye be judged', that the 'tragic position' is a 'painful mystery', in the face of which we should not 'fall back on our everyday legal and moral notions'. In a time when we do not so readily accept everything as the doing of a supreme being, however, it must be valid to examine the facts of history in terms of specifically human actions and man-made institutions, and we may find new insight into the plays if we choose to employ these very 'everyday legal and moral notions', informed by a feeling apprehension of suffering. It is interesting that at points in Bradley's argument, a form of critical analysis does become a possibility:

> When [Cordelia] dies we regard her, practically speaking, simply as we regard Ophelia or Desdemona, as an innocent victim swept away in the convulsion caused by the error or guilt of others.[7]

It is somewhat maddening that the point should be made in such a casual way ('. . . practically speaking, simply . . .'), when its implications challenge Bradley's own avowed refusal to 'judge'. He is judging, to the extent of assuming 'error or guilt', and he is making a far more dangerous value-judgment in his whole procedure of treating the 'others' (if they happen to be tragic heroes) as if they have an exclusive right to the fullest conception of 'tragedy' itself. By and large, Bradley does not follow up the clue he leaves us here. Concerned with examining the 'tragic flaw' of the hero in each play, he rarely looks further at the consequences of the man's actions, nor at the world around him which has its own glaring flaws. Bradley's real sympathies and interest lie in a more complex and psychological suffering which besets the man of state, the 'great man', than in the 'innocent victim'. We do not need, in fact, to deny the prominence of this priority in the plays themselves, but we can argue, as I have done, that the existence of the victims has a definite and important function in attuning our moral sensitivities, checking our complete endorsement of the hero's actions or the norms of a callous world. There is enough circumstantial detail in each play of the consequences for others of the 'error or guilt' of men of power to allow us to interpret the action from this point of view.

There are various ways in which recent critics have sought to explain, or explain away, the moral function of victims in Shakespearean tragedy, and here we draw closer to the two symptomatic quotations with which the section began. One type of critic, after expressing regret and sympathy for a victim, tends to condone the crime by implying that such things 'simply happen', and that it is the strength of the 'realist' or 'pragmatist' that he can accept the way of the world, taking peripheral suffering for granted in a play in which the central protagonist draws so much attention to himself. Kenneth Muir, for example, in his judicious and balanced book on the tragedies, sagely comments on Rymer's distress at the death of Desdemona that 'we can retort that no philosophy or religion is able to protect us from disaster'.[8] Perhaps Keats's 'These things are' is in his mind.[9] But it must be remembered that Keats was speaking of the necessary acceptance of death by some natural means, untimely though it may be. Women have cancers, his brother had a fatal disease of the lungs, and they are cut off in their youth. Desdemona, however, was murdered by another human being, and there is a world of difference. Death itself cannot be philosophized away, particularly if it is some disease or accident which causes it, since it is the fact which defines our mortal condition. But death by some violent means should surely be questioned, even in a 'play', since it cannot be accepted as inevitable or necessary and within the order of nature. One species rarely preys upon its own in nature. Shakespeare's victims do not die of old age or cancer or in an earthquake. Desdemona is murdered as a consequence of the destructiveness of certain male attitudes existing in her society. Lavinia is maimed whilst others are pursuing a brutal ethic of public revenge. Lucrece dies of shame after the crime of rape has been committed against her body and her soul. Ophelia is driven mad by a complex of social, emotional and political conspiracies and deceptions. Cordelia's 'fault' is honestly to resist the arbitrary demands of authority in its most overbearing form, and although she does not die at the hands of her father, she is killed by an equally tyrannical form of authority. Muir, of course, is not attempting to be original here. He is appealing, in fact, to the authority of 'received opinion'. There is something in the tone of critics who believe that Shakespeare is simply uncritically reproducing the normal events of life as we know it, which seeks to persuade us of its rightness by appealing to a notion that the world is, always has been, and always will be, the same. This is certainly an opinion, but not necessarily a truth, and it need not be an opinion that is likely to attract the artist, whose main creative inspiration comes from a belief in the inexhaustible diversity of possibility in people and ideas all over the world. Oscar Wilde's opinion might be equally valid, when he replies to the 'realist's' philosophy:

> *A practical scheme is either a scheme that is already in existence, or a scheme that could be carried out under existing conditions.* But it is exactly the existing conditions that one objects to; and any scheme that could accept these conditions is wrong and foolish. The conditions will be done away with, and human nature will change. The only thing that one really knows about human nature is that it changes. Change is the one quality we can predicate of it . . .[10]

In a somewhat perverse way, the most damaging reply to the argument of the 'realists', who believe that Shakespeare is condoning the way of the world as they know it, exploiting it simply for our 'entertainment' and for our enlightenment about the psychology of great men, comes in an aside from that most maligned critic, Thomas Rymer, who is closer to the pragmatists himself than they will admit. His full statement on Desdemona's death runs thus:

> Rather may we ask here what unnatural crime *Desdemona*, or her Parents had committed, to bring this Judgment down upon her; to Wed a Black-amoor, and innocent to be thus cruelly murder'd by him. What instruction can we make out of this Catastrophe? Or whither must our reflection lead us? Is not this to envenome and sour our spirits, to make us repine and grumble at Providence; and the government of the world? If this be our end, what boots it to be Vertuous?[11]

'Providence' may be something of a red herring, but unless we resort to the sophistical moral dogmas of Rymer himself, there must be in the presentation of the deaths of Desdemona, Ophelia, Cordelia, and the rest, much to 'envenome and sour our spirits, to make us . . . grumble at . . . the government of the World'. Anything short of such galvanized moral attitudes is an insult to Shakespeare's careful presentation of injustice as something we should recognize and resist. In direct answer to Rymer, we may say that his question is wrong. Since it is Othello and Iago rather than any divinity who 'bring this judgement down' upon Desdemona, we should ask 'what unnatural crime have *they* committed?' If the critic chooses to accept and acquiesce in the proposition that every act of injustice is inevitable, unquestionable, and the way of providence in the world, he is not admitting a legitimate area for exploration, either in the play's world or in our own. He certainly cannot argue that Shakespeare has not provided enough evidence of his own horror of injustice in the plays to allow us to examine the issue.

Another way of unconsciously rationalizing injustice in the tragedies, and one that paradoxically owes much to a liberal and open-minded social concern, is to present the tragic hero himself (or even the villain), as the true victim, even when he happens to be a murderer. E.A.J. Honigmann, in his searching and stimulating book on the tragedies, implicitly considers that the most important and interesting problems in 'audience-response' lie in the presentation of the tragic hero. By and large this is irrefutable, simply

because of the amount of attention the dramatist gives to his heroes.
But it should be acknowledged that this is not the only area in which
audience-response operates, and it is at least theoretically possible
that a single, intense moment, such as the reported death of Ophelia,
or Desdemona singing in her bedroom, may inspire resonant responses important for the whole play, if we judge the matter by
quality rather than quantity. Honigmann's book is made up of
profoundly important half-truths, and the other half of the truth is
equally vital. For example, when he says 'Sympathy in the theatre
usually includes elements of approval, even where a villain is
concerned',[12] we must endorse the statement, but we should acknowledge that a part of our response includes the perception that
there are also casualties and victims who suffer at the hands of the
villain himself. No doubt we are swept up by the force of personality
exerted by the protagonist, but we do not altogether forfeit our
critical faculties, particularly when Shakespeare takes so much care
to present us with a fully characterized victim. Although the critic
may carry out deep explorations into 'Lear's Mind', into the 'Secret
Motives of Iago', seeking to understand the sources of this character's evil actions, and he may see Macbeth in the role of 'Murderer as
Victim', we must remember that in each play Shakespeare has also
given us 'The Innocent as Victim' as a strong check on our unequivocal identification with the major, male characters. No doubt
people who hold high office in the militia, the judiciary or any
institution have private feelings and are themselves the victims of
conditioning forces, constraints and preconceptions imposed upon
them by social or psychological factors, but when we witness some
disastrous and murderous consequences for innocent people of their
exercise of power, then 'sympathy', however 'detached', is a
dangerous word. To consistently judge people by their motives
rather than their actions, in literature as in life, may bring us to the
perilous brink of losing all moral bearings and condoning the most
monstrously thoughtless actions, simply because they come from an
authority figure or 'great man'. The road to hell, we presume, is
paved with good intentions. The totality of each play, and the
existence of the victims, prevent us from going over that brink.
Certainly we must be prepared to exercise an emotional responsiveness which is alive to the suffering of the heroes, and to recognize
with fear that 'it could have been us'.[13] But we should equally retain

the wonderfully healthy insights given to us by the moral imagination which cries out that in each play a character whom we may have
grown to love is being treated by society, if not only by a particular
individual, in a repulsively unjust fashion. If we fail to give force to
the latter perception, then we may suddenly find that we are not
judging the plays, but that we have been judged ourselves, and
found somewhat wanting. In this book I hope to have told a different
set of half-truths, in an attempt to redress an imbalance in the critical
accounts of the plays.

To regard the innocent and guilty alike as victims of their social
circumstances and ingrained predilections is a commendable exercise of a broad and humanitarian sympathy, even if such an attitude
tempts us towards a dangerous acceptance of the inevitability of
suffering for the truly innocent, those who commit no moral
transgression but are caught up in a web of destructive circumstances. A truly offensive critical habit, however, is to argue that the
innocents wilfully invite their own deaths by committing some
blatant error themselves. We have encountered such attitudes when
looking in detail at each play, and for the moment, in order to repeat
the broad point, I can do little better than quote again from Harriett
Hawkins:

> . . . our libraries are full of discussions of Elizabethan drama
> which 'go so far as virtually to deny that any of the sufferers in a
> tragedy is innocent', and which blame 'the errors and misdoings
> of major and minor characters alike' for their tragic fates. [Quot-
> ing from Helen Gardner, *Religion and Literature*] Any weakness or
> peccadillo is enough to subject a character to critical cords and
> whips. There are long essays about the misdemeanours of the
> Duchess of Malfi and the indiscretions of Desdemona . . .[14]

She goes on to quote one example, a critic who suggests that in
interpreting the characters of Desdemona and Juliet 'we must allow
for the weight given by Shakespeare to the sin of disobedience to
parents . . .'[15] Hawkins continues:

> And so it goes, on and on, in essay after essay, book after book.
> Desdemona and Juliet disobey their fathers — off with their
> heads! The Duchess of Malfi defies her brother — off with hers.
> Yet modern critics who rail against the 'sin' of 'disobedience' to

parents and other authorities conveniently overlook the obvious fact that, in his comedies, Shakespeare gives such 'sins' no weight whatsoever.

This is certainly one powerful argument against the sternly authoritarian critics, but there are others. For example, Ophelia dies partly because she has *not* disobeyed her father. There are others such as Lavinia, Lucrece, and children, who cannot under any circumstances be regarded as disobeying any moral code whatsoever. Finally, and crucially, to harp on disobedience to authority in such cases allows only one side into the argument, for it is the fathers and the kings themselves who tell us of the existence of a sin. Lear acts as aggressor, prosecutor and judge over Cordelia, and will not even listen to his loyal (but presumably equally 'disobedient') courtier, Kent. We, as audience, need not ignore Kent, nor the whole context in which Cordelia commits her 'sin'. One associates the tendency to blame victims for their own fates with critics of previous centuries, but the tiny quotations examined at the beginning of this chapter, as well as the examples given by Hawkins, show that more recently the habit is to make such accusations in a 'by the way' manner, as explication of the text rather than explicitly. They are no less questionable, however, for the unobtrusiveness of presentation.

Behind many of the subtle techniques of academic rationalization of the victims in the tragedies, and particularly the one that seeks to blame them for their own misfortunes, lies in a shadowy way a doctrine which is so pervasive in western society that few bother even to mention it. It is not impossible to find reasons for critical attempts to trace all deaths indiscriminately in a play back to 'original sin', since much of our culture and literary experience encourages us to do so. When we speak of 'poetic justice' in the case of tragic heroes or tragic villains, we are imputing to the literary world a concept of some form of retributive justice which assumes that death itself is a punishment, and therefore, since it is inevitable for everybody at some time, a proof of the existence of original sin in even the most apparently innocent. With the possible exception of Hamlet, we can say of Shakespeare's major protagonists, as of Oedipus, that their suffering is related directly to their own past actions, and however excessive the form of punishment may seem in some cases, we can find a certain appropriateness in it. It is tempting to extend such a principle consistently to cover other characters who suffer and die in the plays, but if we do so, we are on uncertain ground. As we have seen, some critics over the centuries have argued that such characters as Ophelia, Desdemona and Cordelia die as a consequence of their own sins and misdeeds. Behind such an argument lies a philosophy that Nietzsche associated with Christian teaching in particular, the notion that misfortune is associated with guilt:

> . . . it was reserved for Christianity to say: 'Here is a great misfortune and behind it there *must* lie hidden a great, *equally great* guilt, even though it may not be clearly visible! If you, unfortunate man, do not feel this you are *obdurate* — you will have to suffer worse things!' — Moreover, in antiquity there still existed actual misfortune, pure innocence; only in Christendom did everything become punishment, well-deserved punishment.[16]

We cannot really know that the classical world was so free of the concept of well-deserved punishment for all, if only because nowadays we must read Sophocles and Aristotle with Shakespeare and Christian teachings in our minds. But Nietzsche's ironic characterization of the attitude which equates misfortune with punishment imposed by God as a judgment is a salutary warning when we come to examine the misfortunes of our 'innocent victims'. If we pay sensitive attention both to the dramatic personalities of these characters and to the way they are treated by others in the plays, then we can only condemn such an assumption of culpability as a failure of perception as much as failure of the moral imagination. It is a possible position in such a debate to argue that Shakespeare is telling us that at least some (and perhaps all) people are born innocent rather than sinful, that much of the suffering in the world is unnecessary, and can be traced back past individuals to the existence of authority, some general attitudes, and state institutions. (To this extent, at least, we *can* validly see characters such as Iago, Edmund and Macbeth as 'victims', if not innocent ones.) The truly innocent victims are presented as such by Shakespeare, and they die as a direct consequence of the careless or vindictive actions of others. They are caught up in a mesh of circumstances created by the existence of evil attitudes in their own societies, and the fact that these societies seek to cover up the crimes should tell us more about the fundamental evils, rather than allowing us easily to acquiesce in their ignorances and justifications.

To be quite fair to theologians, the popular notion of 'original sin' as paraphrased by Nietzsche is not necessarily true to the evidence in the Bible, and other perfectly reputable interpretations have been proposed which offer support for the argument in this book.[17] The popular notion, I take it, is that since Adam sinned we are all sinful, and must, like Pilgrim, carry our pack of sins on our backs from the moment of birth.

Using evidence from the Bible, other commentators have proposed that Adam's sin was representative of mankind as a general entity rather than attaching necessarily to people as individuals. The implications of this theory are interesting, and I find them more compassionate and consistent. If Adam introduced sin into the world then each individual, although born innocent, must cope with a wicked world by exercising a genuine moral choice about his or her actions. 'Freedom of choice' then becomes a genuine reality. Furthermore, the sin which we find in the world, in order to survive and predate individuals, must reside in continuing entities such as institutions which cannot be said to be the individual creation or responsibility of a single person. In terms of this book, we should say that once a character such as Macbeth or Richard III (to take obvious examples) equate themselves with an institution like kingship or the state, then they forfeit a large element of their individuality and their innocence. They have, by exercising a moral choice, 'fallen' and thereafter they are agents for perpetuating the sins of the fallen world which victimizes the innocent. When Lear chooses to place 'authority' of a king and a father higher than feelings, he 'falls', and so does Othello when he equates himself with an abstract concept like divine justice. As a *coda*, it might be clearer to describe the two rival notions of original sin in the following way. The popular view is that the garden of Eden is irretrievably gone from the world of mortality. The second view is that we are given the benefit of beginning in the paradise of innocence (and who would argue that even the noisiest, most demanding new-born infant is actually *evil?*), and we are later turned out into the world much as a bird is forced to leave the nest, in order to confront its adversities and learn from them, always carrying with us our intuitive, paradisal knowledge of good. It is interesting that John Keats, in forging his own, unique philosophy of life, reaches a curiously similar position even as he rejects conventional religious teaching on the world as a 'vale of tears':

> Call the world if you Please 'The vale of Soul-making' Then you will find out the use of the world . . . I will call the *world* a School instituted for the purpose of teaching little children to read — I will call the *human heart* the *horn Book* used in that School — and I will call the *child able to read, the Soul* made from that *school* and its *hornbook*. Do you not see how necessary a World of Pains and troubles is to school an Intelligence and make it a soul? A Place where the heart must feel and suffer in a thousand diverse ways![18]

It should once again be stressed that Keats in talking of adversity is thinking of the inevitability of suffering and death, and given his strong commitment to benevolent action he would admit the notion that the fully formed 'Soul' or identity may use 'the proovings of his heart'[19] to fight against things like cruelty and victimization in order to change the world for the better. My reading of Shakespeare's tragedies would make them comparable to Keats's 'horn Book' in which the dramatist awakens in us and trains a conscious moral indignation at the sight of cruelty directed at the innocent. The plays then become as consistently educative as any neo-classical theorist would wish.

There is always a temptation to turn a blind eye to the plight of innocent victims, and to demean the importance of their existence by any one of various attitudes such as sentimentality, rationalization, embarrassed condescension or simple dismissiveness. Shakespeare, by keeping his eye always on the object of human behaviour, never falls into the error. As critics of Shakespeare, (and every audience and reader stands in the position of critic), we should train ourselves anew in his uncompromising, deeply moral and unflinching modes of perception. The tired impasse into which contemporary Shakespearean criticism has been led by its constant insistence upon the old questions (Hamlet's 'madness', Lear's 'resurrection', Othello's 'jealousy', and so on) should be rejected in favour of a fresher, more relevant approach, which can find immediate, human touchstones for evaluating and understanding the plays. A lot more can be said, in different voices, about Shakespeare's innocent victims, than can be acknowledged in such a book as this. I hope the challenge will be taken up.

Notes

I Fore Thoughts

1 Oscar Wilde, *The Importance of Being Earnest*.
2 E.A.J. Honigmann, *Shakespeare: Seven Tragedies: The Dramatist's Manipulation of Response* (London, 1976), p. 198.
3 Shelley, *A Defence of Poetry*.
4 Especially the wife of Hieronomo in *The Spanish Tragedy* (IV.ii). It is tempting to say that Kyd's treatment of her provides Shakespeare with his paradigm. For the general treatment of justice in *The Spanish Tragedy* see 'Ironies of Justice in *The Spanish Tragedy*', reprinted in G.K. Hunter, *Dramatic Identities and Cultural Tradition* (Liverpool, 1978).
5 Harriett Hawkins, *Poetic Freedom and Poetic Truth* (Oxford, 1976), p. 25.
6 Quotations from Shakespeare are taken from Peter Alexander, *William Shakespeare: The Complete Works* (London and Glasgow, 1951).

II Innocent Victims

1 Keats, 'On Sitting Down to Read *King Lear* Once Again'.
2 Hawkins, *Poetic Freedom*, p. 13.
3 *Bertholt Brecht: Poems*, ed. John Willett and Ralph Mannheim (London, 1976), p. 452.
4 Sophocles, *The Theban Plays*, translated E.F. Watling (Harmondsworth, 1947).
5 I borrow Lewis Carroll's phrase in this context via Harriett Hawkins, *Poetic Freedom*, p. 27 (quoted in full on page 128).
6 *Romeo and Juliet*, III.i.103.
7 The phrase is from Gamini Salgado, *The Elizabethan Underworld* (London, 1977), p. 199.
8 For a most interesting opinion on Shakespeare's own bias, see Edward Bond's essay, 'The Rational Theatre' in *Plays: Two* (London, 1978).
9 Hunter, *Dramatic Identities*, p. 236.

III Lavinia

1 The phrase is used by Kenneth Muir in *Shakespeare's Tragic Sequence* (London, 1972), p. 20.
2 R.S. White, 'Hunting in Shakespearean Comedy', *Durham University Journal* lxix (1976).
3 See G.K. Hunter's most penetrating comments in 'Seneca and the

Elizabethans' and 'Seneca and English Tragedy', both reprinted in *Dramatic Identities.*

4 Hunter, *Dramatic Identities*, p. 166.

IV *Lucrece*

1 J.C. Maxwell writes in the New Cambridge edition (Cambridge, 1966), pp. xxi and xxiii: 'But what is important about Shakespeare's rehandling of the story is not his use of earlier versions in detail, but the radically different impressions that his poem as a whole makes. Not only is it greatly expanded, but it displays a type of interest in the figure of Tarquin that is quite new. It is here, rather than in the story of Lucrece, that the poem points significantly forward to later Shakespearian tragedy . . . As Fr Christopher Devlin puts it, Shakespeare "is more concerned with Tarquin's soul than Lucrece's body." ' See also F.T. Prince in the Arden edition (London, 1960), p. xxxvi. These critics exemplify an almost universal reading of the poem. But contrast Harold R. Walley, '*The Rape of Lucrece* and Shakespearean Tragedy', *PMLA* lxxvi (1961). Walley's understanding of the tragic pattern is closer to the one presented in this book, and he writes, 'Essentially *Lucrece* is an examination of what constitutes tragedy and an exploration of how it happens' (p. 487).

2 See D.C. Allen in 'Some Observations on *The Rape of Lucrece*', *Shakespeare Survey* xv (1962), reprinted in *Image and Meaning* (Baltimore, second edition, 1968). For a comprehensive account of the varying treatments of the Lucrece myth, see the excellent book by Ian Donaldson, *The Rapes of Lucretia: A Myth and its Transformations* (Oxford, 1982).

3 See P.W. Miller, 'The Elizabethan Minor Epic', *Studies in Philology*, lv (1958).

4 'The Ironic Reading of *The Rape of Lucrece* and the Problem of External Evidence', *Shakespeare Survey*, 34 (1981), pp. 85–92.

5 An interesting, recent commentary on the poem, and one which touches on some of the points made here, is by Clark Hulse, *Metamorphic Verse: The Elizabethan Minor Epic* (Princeton, 1981).

V *Children*

1 The next scene (IV.iii) clarifies the nature of the moral debate in which we have been involved. Malcolm, as he suddenly considers the possibility that he will be the next king, imaginatively finds within himself the terrible capacities of a murderer and rapist, in a nightmare vision that puts even Macbeth's crimes into the pale. We recall that it was Macbeth's imagination, activated by the concurrence of events when he met the witches and was immediately promoted by the king to within 'striking distance' of the throne, which impelled him towards the

murders, both personal and vicarious, culminating in the death of the child. We recall also that both the Thane of Cawdor and Macbeth himself had proved themselves totally trustworthy and virtuous, before their aspirations compelled them to imagine power. Macduff, the honest, straightforward man at first disbelieves Malcolm's horrifying revery (comparable in every way to Macbeth's 'raptness'), until at last he rejects Malcolm as fit 'not to live', whereupon Malcolm awakes from his imaginative vision and expediently reassures him. In other words, it is power itself, and the imaginative awareness that high office is within grasp, which allows a man to find the capacity for evil, violence and corruption in his own personality. There is evidence in the play that if power itself, as an institutional licence for evil, did not exist, then human beings would not contemplate murder and corrupt actions. It is essential to the design of the play that we do not realize this for a long time, as we participate in Macbeth's imaginings, but it is even more essential to the *moral* design that we are forced to 'wake up' in these two scenes. If we do not, then the play fails in its palpable, morally educative function: or rather, *we* have failed in the exercise of our moral sensibilities.

2   E.g. see the translation by Paul Turner (Harmondsworth, 1965), pp. 47–9 and 128–9, where questions of political and economic injustice are most directly analysed.

3   See Thomas Campbell, *Life of Mrs Siddons* (2 vols. 1834), I, 215 ff.

4   E.A.J. Honigmann (ed.) Arden edition of *King John* (London, fourth edition, 1954), p. lxvii.

5   R.L. Smallwood, (ed.) Penguin edition of *King John*, (Harmondsworth, 1974), pp. 36 ff.

VI Ophelia

1   Dame Rebecca West, quoted by Harold Jenkins in 'Hamlet and Ophelia', *British Academy Lectures* 49 (1963), p. 135. Even the priest burying Ophelia may believe this, if we take the force of the pun on 'strumpet' (a device used by Shakespeare in *Troilus and Cressida*, 'The Troyans' trumpet', (IV.v.63)):
> She should in ground unsanctified have lodg'd
> Till the last trumpet.
>   (v.i.223–4)

2   This point is made most clearly by Nigel Alexander in *Poison, Play and Duel* (London, 1971).

3   Keats to Fanny Brawne, August (?), 1820.

4   *Works of Samuel Johnson*, ed. Arthur Sherbo (New Haven, 1968), viii, p. 1011.

5   *Passages from the Prose and Table Talk of Coleridge*, ed. W.H. Dircks (London, 1894), p. 202.

6   Robert Burton, *The Anatomy of Melancholy*, ed. H. Jackson (London, 1932), Third Partition, Memb. 3.
7   Alexander, *Poison*, p. 129.
8   H. Goddard, 'In Ophelia's Closet', *Yale Review* xxxv (1945), pp. 462–74.
9   Jenkins, 'Hamlet and Ophelia', and J.M. Nosworthy, 'Hamlet and the Pangs of Love', *Elizabethan Theatre IV*, ed. G.R. Hibbard (Toronto, 1974), pp. 41–56. See also Leo Kirschbaum, 'Hamlet and Ophelia', *Philological Quarterly* xxxv (1956), pp. 376–93 and C.J. Carlisle, 'Cruelty in the Nunnery Scene', *Shakespeare Quarterly* xvii (1967), pp. 129–40.
10 For example, see *Much Ado About Nothing*, ii.i.193: 'and I off'red him my company to a willow tree, either to make him a garland, as being forsaken . . .'
11 See J. Dover Wilson (ed.), *Hamlet* (Cambridge, 1936), p. 231.
12 See A.C. Bradley, *Shakespearean Tragedy* (second edition, London, 1905), pp. 407–9.
13 This phrase may now confidently be used as a term of art since the book by Francis Berry, *The Shakespearean Inset* (London, 1965).

VII Desdemona

1   But it is noticeable that Shakespeare does make changes: in Cinthio, Desdemona is killed by being struck on the skull by both male protagonists, after which they simulate an accident by pulling down the ceiling. Shakespeare did not, then, accept some things as inevitable simply because they were in his source.
2   Quoted in Geoffrey Tillotson's *Essays in Criticism and Research* (Cambridge, 1942), ' "Othello" and "The Alchemist" at Oxford in 1610'.
3   Johnson probably also found the line inconsistent with the earlier one: '*Desdemona*: That death's unnatural that kills for loving.' (v.ii.45)
4   Variorum *Othello*, ed. H.H. Furness (Philadelphia, 1886), p. 300, fn. 80.
5   Bradley, *Shakespearean Tragedy*, p. 203.
6   The critical disagreements over the evaluation of Othello's personality (which I frankly find a barren debate), can of course be traced from the comments of T.S. Eliot in *Selected Essays* (1932) and F.R. Leavis in *The Common Pursuit* (1952), and in the plethora of critical writings they have stimulated.
7   John Bayley, *The Characters of Love* (London, 1960), chapter 3 *passim*. I still find this essay the most satisfactory on the play, together with Bradley's chapter and G. Wilson Knight's 'The Othello Music' in *The Wheel of Fire* (London, 1949).
8   *Troilus and Cressida* (iv.v.56). For some sensitive comments on the dilemmas of Cressida, see John Bayley, *The Uses of Division: Unity and Disharmony in Literature* (London, 1976).

9 For useful accounts of this aspect of the play, see G.K. Hunter, 'Othello and Colour Prejudice', reprinted in *Dramatic Identities* and Helen Gardner, 'The Noble Moor', *Proceedings of the British Academy* xli (1955).

10 This statement will be found tendentious by those who agree with the Leavis–Eliot approach. It is my consistent assertion that Othello *changes* during the course of the play, that he is partly redeemed at the end by his recognition of guilt, and that he 'learns' something from his murder of Desdemona. Iago, in contrast, confesses no guilt, and his moral degradation is complete.

11 Quoted in the Variorum *Othello*, p. 413.

12 The phrase is reported to us by Severn. See *The Keats Circle*, ed. H.E. Rollins (Cambridge, Mass., 1958), ii. pp. 134–5.

13 The aptness of the comparison is best established by quoting:

> Thus was this monster by the maystring might
> Of doughty Calidore, supprest and tamed,
> That neuer more he mote endammadge wight
> With his vile tongue, which many had defamed,
> And many causelesse caused to be blamed:
> So did he eekelong after this remaine,
> Vntill that, whether wicked fate so framed,
> Or fault of men, he broke his yron chaine,
> And got into the world at liberty againe.
>   (*The Faerie Queene*, vi.xii.38. See also 39, 40)

VIII Cordelia

1 From Johnson's comment on *King Lear*, most conveniently available in *Shakespeare Criticism 1623–1840*, selected D. Nichol Smith (Oxford, 1916), p. 120.

2 S.L. Goldberg, *An Essay on King Lear* (Cambridge, 1974), p. 22. Goldberg's broad attitude to the scene is that 'Two wrongs don't make a right' (p. 28). But his book is far too subtle and perceptive to reduce in such a fashion. Perhaps the most extreme example of a critic seeking to find fault in Cordelia is tucked away in a footnote to R.B. Heilman's *This Great Stage: Image and Structure in 'King Lear'* (Washington, 1963) where the writer says that Cordelia bears 'an ancillary responsibility for the career of Goneril and Regan' (p. 300), a judgment which seems to lack not only compassion but logical reasonableness. However Cordelia had acted, there is at least a strong chance that she would still have been destroyed in the same way. As usual, the critic is seeking to justify in detail an overall thesis which ends up making Cordelia into the same *kind* of tragic figure (although a 'secondary' one) as Lear: 'the immaculateness of nonparticipation must be balanced against action which may bespot the actor but is yet a responsibility' (p. 36). Despite his perfunctory and schematic treatment of the role of Cordelia, Heilman's book presents a strong argument which must be taken note of. See also the

lengthy and challenging account of 'natural justice' in Wilson Knight's *The Wheel of Fire.*

3 For a thorough study of invocations in *King Lear* see 'The Technique of Invocation in *King Lear*' by J.C. Maxwell, *Modern Language Review* xlv (1950).

4 The reader may need reminding that Shakespeare has altered his sources in making the play into a tragedy. See especially Geoffrey Bullough, *Narrative and Dramatic Sources of Shakespeare*, vol. vii (London, 1973), pp. 309–402 *passim.*

5 Of the criticism devoted to the Fool's capacities for reason, one might single out the chapter in John F. Danby's *Shakespeare's Doctrine of Nature: A Study of King Lear* (London, 1949). Enid Welsford in *The Fool* (London, 1935) writes: Lear's Fool 'is in fact the sage-fool who sees the truth, and his role has even more *intellectual* than emotional significance' (p. 253). The notes to Dr Johnson's edition (or a thorough modern edition) show the rational outlook behind the Fool's statements.

6 A brief but interesting approach comes from Ralph Berry in 'Woman as Fool: Dramatic Mechanism in Shakespeare' in *Shakespearean Structures* (London, 1981).

IX After Thoughts

1 The reader of a jurisprudential turn of mind may wish to consult on these matters John Rawls, *A Theory of Justice* (Oxford, 1972) and John Finnis, *Natural Law and Natural Rights* (Oxford, 1980).

2 John Bayley, *Shakespeare and Tragedy* (London, 1980).

Appendix: Critics and Victims

1 Nicholas Brooke, *Shakespeare's Early Tragedies* (London, 1968), p. 33.

2 Brooke, *Early Tragedies*, p. 46 and *passim.*

3 Clifford Leech, *Shakespeare's Tragedies and Other Studies in Seventeenth Century Drama* (London, 1950), pp. 75–6.

4 From Johnson's *Preface to Shakespeare* (1765). See Nichol Smith, *Shakespeare Criticism*, p. 88.

5 See especially Lawrence's essays 'Why the Novel Matters' and 'Morality and the Novel', available in *D.H. Lawrence, Selected Literary Criticism*, ed. Anthony Beal (London, 1956).

6 Letter to Woodhouse, 27 October 1818.

7 *Shakespearean Tragedy*, p. 270. See also pp. 22–9. It is fashionable these days to dismiss Bradley for one reason or another. I suspect this tendency is because some of his admirers (who usually emphasize only certain strengths) and his denigrators have simply not *read* Bradley, or at least have not read him for some time. If we read him carefully, I believe that we discover that he is never so simple-minded as critics often present him, that his subtle mind has answered virtually every

criticism that has been made of him, and that amongst the extraordinary range of his perceptions we find anticipations of major schools of twentieth-century Shakespeare criticism. In short, I believe his work still to be unsurpassed, and the criticism made of him in this chapter should be regarded in the light of this judgment.

8 Kenneth Muir, *Shakespeare's Tragic Sequence* (London, 1972). p. 115. On p. 138, Muir writes: 'A dramatist who pretended that only the wicked suffer in this life would be immoral because he would know that his picture of life was a false one'. Perhaps this is true if we take 'false' with a mimetic rather than moral content, but it would seem more important to stress that the dramatist would indeed be immoral if he did not demonstrate and implicitly condemn the injustice of the death of innocents. Muir may even mean this, but he never says so. I am aware of Professor Muir's moving answer to the charge of 'complacent acceptance of suffering' in *Critical Quarterly*, iii (1961), and although he may be right in not intruding personal views into *editorial* work it is a shame he did not take the opportunity of his *critical* book to express more of his feelings about Cordelia and Desdemona. Such feelings, I would guess, are more universal than personal.

9 Keats wrote to Benjamin Bailey on 23 January 1818 as follows: '. . . "*Why should Woman suffer?*" Aye. Why should she? "By heavens I'd coin my Soul and drop my Blood for Drachmas"! These things are, and he who feels how incompetent the most skyey Knight errantry/is/to heal this bruised fairness is like a sensitive leaf on the hot hand of thought.' Quoted from the edition of Keats's Letters by Hyder Rollins, 2 vols (Cambridge, Mass., 1958), i.209.

10 Oscar Wilde, *The Soul of Man Under Socialism*.

11 Rymer, *A Short View of Tragedy*, quoted by Clifford Leech in *Shakespeare's Tragedies*, p. 103.

12 E.A.J. Honigmann, *Shakespeare. Seven Tragedies. The Dramatist's Manipulation of Response* (London, 1976), p. 23.

13 See R.B. Heilman, 'The Criminal as Tragic Hero', *Shakespeare Survey* xix (1966). My real quarrel with this group of critics is not in terms of their central thesis, which I implicitly support in discussing sympathy for the tragic hero in the chapter on 'Innocent Victims'. Rather, it is with their failure to do justice to the ways in which Shakespeare at certain times *disengages* our sympathies, allowing us to exert what Bradley once calls a 'healthy moral sense'. This is largely done by the attention drawn to the victim's undeserved plight.

14 Hawkins, *Poetic Freedom*, p. 26.

15 Ibid.

16 Quoted in *A Nietzsche Reader*, ed. R.J. Hollingdale (Harmondsworth, 1977), p. 176.

17 I am very grateful to Dr Mark Corner of the Department of Religious Studies in the University of Newcastle upon Tyne for guiding me through some of the shoals of commentary on original sin, although any errors or misunderstandings in what I have said are entirely my

own fault. I found helpful the books by John Hicks, *Evil and the Love of God* (London, 1966), and W.D. Davies, *Paul and Rabbinic Judaism* (London, 1970).

18   Keats, *Letters* ii, 102.
19   Ibid.

Bibliography

Although each of the works listed below was in some way relevant to the writing of this book, only some of them complement, in part or in whole, the argument presented here. I have found nothing systematic written along the lines of my approach, although many critics offer hints and glimpses, perhaps especially in the eighteenth century when analysis based on a moral understanding was more acceptable, if at times it was also constricting. Items below under Dollimore and Lenz indicate that more will be said along similar lines in future. Editions of plays listed under the editor's name have been included because of helpful critical/introductory matter rather than for textual reasons.

General

Roy W. Battenhouse, *Shakespearean Tragedy: Its Art and Its Christian Premises* (Bloomington and London, 1969).

John Bayley, *The Uses of Division: Unity and Disharmony in Literature* (London, 1976).

John Bayley, *Shakespeare and Tragedy* (London, 1981).

A.C. Bradley, *Shakespearean Tragedy* (second edition, London, 1905).

Francis Berry, *The Shakespearean Inset* (London, 1965).

Edward Bond, 'The Rational Theatre' and 'Author's Preface' to *Lear* in *Plays: Two* (London, 1978)

Robert Burton, *The Anatomy of Melancholy*, ed. H. Jackson (London, 1932).

S.T. Coleridge, *Passages from the Prose and Table Talk of Coleridge*, ed. W.H. Dircks (London, 1894).

W.D. Davies, *Paul and Rabbinic Judaism* (London, 1970).

Jonathon Dollimore, *Radical Tragedy: Religion, Ideology and Power in the Drama of Shakespeare and his Contemporaries* (Brighton, 1983).

Juliet Dusinberre, *Shakespeare and the Nature of Women* (New York and London, 1975).

John Finniss, *Natural Law and Natural Rights* (Oxford, 1980).

Harriett Hawkins, *Poetic Freedom and Poetic Truth* (Oxford, 1976).

William Hazlitt, *Characters of Shakespeare's Plays* (London, 1817).

R.B. Heilman, 'The Criminal as Tragic Hero', *Shakespeare Survey*, xix (1966).

John Hicks, *Evil and the Love of God* (London, 1966).

E.A.J. Honigmann, *Shakespeare. Seven Tragedies. The Dramatist's Manipulation of Response* (London, 1976).

G.K. Hunter, *Dramatic Identities and Cultural Tradition* (Liverpool, 1978).

Samuel Johnson, *Works*, ed. Arthur Sherbo (New Haven, 1968), viii.

Coppelia Kahn, *Man's Estate: Male Identity in Shakespeare* (Berkeley, 1980).

Clifford Leech, *Shakespeare's Tragedies and Other Studies in Seventeenth-century Drama* (London, 1950).

C.R.S. Lenz, G. Greene and C.T. Neely (eds), *The Woman's Part: Feminist Criticism of Shakespeare* (Urbana, 1980).

Kenneth Muir, *Shakespeare's Tragic Sequence* (London, 1972).

F. Nietzsche, *A Nietzsche Reader*, ed. R.J. Hollingdale (Harmondsworth, 1977).

John Rawls, *A Theory of Justice* (Oxford, 1972).

Gamini Salgado, *The Elizabethan Underworld* (London, 1977).

Shakespeare, *The Complete Works*, ed. Peter Alexander (London and Glasgow, 1951).

Shelley, *A Defence of Poetry* (written 1821, published 1840).

Oscar Wilde, *The Soul of Man Under Socialism* (1891).

Lavinia

Nicholas Brooke, *Shakespeare's Early Tragedies* (London, 1968).

J.C. Maxwell (ed.) *Titus Andronicus* (London, third edition, 1953).

Edward Ravenscroft, *Titus Andronicus, or the Rape of Lavinia* (London, 1867). A rewriting of the play, significant for the emphasis on Lavinia in the title.

Catharine R. Stimpson, 'Shakespeare and the Soil of Rape', in Lenz, Greene and Neely (eds.), *The Woman's Part*.

David Willbern, 'Rape and Revenge in *Titus Andronicus*', *English Literary Renaissance*, viii (1978).

Lucrece

D.C. Allen, 'Some Observations on *The Rape of Lucrece*', *Shakespeare Survey*, xv (1962), reprinted in *Image and Meaning* (Baltimore, second edition, 1968).

Ian Donaldson, *The Rapes of Lucretia: A Myth and its Transformations* (Oxford, 1982).

Clarke Hulse, *Metamorphic Verse: The Elizabethan Minor Epic* (Princeton, 1981).

Coppelia Kahn, 'The Rape of Shakespeare's Lucrece', *Shakespeare Studies*, ix (1976).

Richard Levin, 'The Ironic Reading of *The Rape of Lucrece* and the Problem of External Evidence', *Shakespeare Survey* 34 (1981).

J.C. Maxwell (ed.), *The Poems of Shakespeare* (Cambridge, 1966).

P.W. Miller, 'The Elizabethan Minor Epic', *Studies in Philology*, lv (1958).

Stimpson, 'Shakespeare and the Soil of Rape'.

Harold R. Walley, '*The Rape of Lucrece* and Shakespearean Tragedy,' *PMLA* (lxxvi (1961).

Children

Cleanth Brooks, 'The Naked Babe and the Cloak of Manliness', in *The Well-Wrought Urn* (New York, 1947).

E.A.J. Honigmann (ed.), *King John* (London, fourth edition, 1954).

E.A.J. Honigmann (ed.), *Richard III* (Harmondsworth, 1968).

G.K. Hunter, (ed.), *Macbeth* (Harmondsworth, 1967).

Kenneth Muir (ed.), *Macbeth* (London, ninth edition, 1952).

R.L. Smallwood (ed.), *King John* (Harmondsworth, 1974).

Richard Wheeler, 'History, Character and Conscience in *Richard III*', *Comparative Drama*, v (1971–2).

Ophelia   BUSCAR BIBLIOTECA

Nigel Alexander, *Poison, Play and Duel* (London, 1971).

C.J. Carlisle, 'Cruelty in the Nunnery Scene', *Shakespeare Quarterly*, xvii (1967).

Harold Goddard, 'In Ophelia's Closet', *Yale Review*, xxxv (1945).

*Copiar la bibliografía porc
buscarla en España si no
estén aquí*

Harold Jenkins, 'Hamlet and Ophelia', *British Academy Lectures*, 49 (1963).

Leo Kirschbaum, 'Hamlet and Ophelia', *Philological Quarterly*, xxxv (1956).

William W. Lawrence, 'Ophelia's Heritage', *MLR*, xlii (1947).

B.G. Lyons, 'The Iconography of Ophelia', *English Literary History*, xliv (1977).

J.M. Nosworthy, 'Hamlet and the Pangs of Love', *Elizabethan Theatre IV*, ed. G.R. Hibbard (Toronto, 1974).

John E. Seaman, 'The "Rose of May" in the Unweeded Garden', *Etudes Anglaises*, xxii (1969).

L.W. Wagner, 'Ophelia: Shakespeare's Pathetic Plot Device', *Shakespeare Quarterly*, xiv (1963).

J. Dover Wilson (ed.), *Hamlet* (Cambridge, 1936).

Desdemona

Jane Adamson, *Othello as Tragedy: Some Problems of Judgement and Feeling* (Cambridge, 1980).

John Bayley, *The Characters of Love* (London, 1960).

G. Bonnard, 'Are Othello and Desdemona innocent or Guilty?', *English Studies*, xxx (1949). (The verdict is 'Guilty'.)

Carroll Camden, 'Iago on Women', *JEGP*, xlviii (1949).

Barbara Everett, 'Reflections on the Sentimentalist's Othello', *Critical Quarterly*, iii (1961).

H.H. Furness (ed.), *Othello* (Philadelphia, 1886).

Helen Gardner, 'The Noble Moor', *Proceedings of the British Academy*, xli (1955).

S.N. Garner, 'Shakespeare's Desdemona', *Shakespeare Studies*, ix (1976).

Arthur Kirsch, 'The Polarization of Erotic Love in *Othello*', *Modern Language Review*, 73 (1978).

G. Wilson Knight, *The Wheel of Fire* (London, 1949).

F.R. Leavis, 'The Diabolic Intellect and the Noble Hero', *The Common Pursuit* (London, 1952).

Carol T. Neely, 'Women and Men in *Othello*: "What should such a fool/Do with so good a woman" ', in Lenz, Greene and Neely (eds), in *The Woman's Part*.

W. Nowottny, 'Justice and Love in Othello', *University of Toronto Quarterly*, xxi (1952).

M.L. Ranald, 'The Indiscretions of Desdemona', *Shakespeare Quarterly*, xiv (1963).

Thomas Rymer, *A Short View of Tragedy* (1693).

Geoffrey Tillotson, '*Othello* and *The Alchemist* at Oxford in 1610', *Essays in Criticism and Research* (Cambridge, 1942).

Alice Walker and J. Dover Wilson (eds), *Othello* (Cambridge, 1957).

Cordelia

Ralph Berry, 'Woman as Fool: Dramatic Mechanism in Shakespeare', *Shakespearean Structures* (London, 1981).

John F. Danby, *Shakespeare's Doctrine of Nature: A Study of King Lear* (London, 1949).

J.P. Driscoll, 'The Vision of King Lear', *Shakespeare Studies*, x (1977).

Barbara Everett, 'The New King Lear', *Critical Quarterly*, ii (1960).

S.L. Goldberg, *An Essay on King Lear* (Cambridge, 1974).

R.B. Heilman, *This Great Stage: Image and Structure in 'King Lear'* (Washington, 1963).

Arnold Isenberg, 'Cordelia Absent', *Shakespeare Quarterley*, ii (1951).

J.C. Maxwell, 'The Technique of Invocation in *King Lear*', *Modern Language Review*, xlv (1950).

Ivor Morris, 'Cordelia and Lear', *Shakespeare Quarterley*, viii (1957).

Kenneth Muir (ed.), *King Lear* (London, eighth edition, 1952).

T.B. Stroup, 'Cordelia and the Fool', *Shakespeare Quarterly*, xii (1961).

Index